AF228545

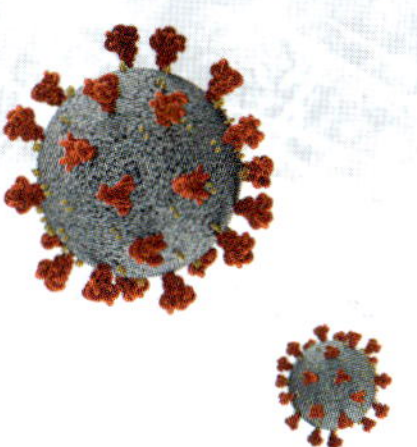

FIGHTING COVID-19 IN THE UNITED STATES

BY HEIDI DEAL

CONTENT CONSULTANT

Kevin M. Bakker, PhD
Assistant Research Scientist
Department of Epidemiology
School of Public Health
University of Michigan

Essential Library

An Imprint of Abdo Publishing
abdobooks.com

ABDOBOOKS.COM

Published by Abdo Publishing, a division of ABDO, PO Box 398166, Minneapolis, Minnesota 55439. Copyright © 2023 by Abdo Consulting Group, Inc. International copyrights reserved in all countries. No part of this book may be reproduced in any form without written permission from the publisher. Essential Library™ is a trademark and logo of Abdo Publishing.

Printed in the United States of America, North Mankato, Minnesota.
052022
092022

Cover Photo: Shutterstock Images
Interior Photos: Ken Cedeno/Abaca Press/Sipa USA/AP Images, 4; Elaine Thompson/AP Images, 9; National Photo Company Collection/Library of Congress, 14; Craig Lassig/AP Images, 16; Sgt. John Schoebel/US Army National Guard/AP Images, 22; Red Line Editorial, 25, 52; Matt Stone/Boston Herald/MediaNews Group/Getty Images, 26; Salvatore Di Nolfi/Keystone/AP Images, 28; Jim Lo Scalzo/Getty Images News/Getty Images, 33; Shutterstock Images, 34, 55, 56; Michael Reynolds/EPA/AP Images, 37; Mandel Ngan/AFP/Getty Images, 40; John Minchillo/AP Images, 46; Carlos Osorio/AP Images, 58; Tom Williams/CQ-Roll Call Inc./Getty Images, 64; Erik Kabik Photography/MediaPunch/IPX/AP Images, 69; Mark J. Terrill/AP Images, 71; Jeffrey Greenberg/Education Images/Universal Images Group/Getty Images, 73; Amanda Andrade-Rhoades/The Washington Post/Getty Images, 74; Rogelio V. Solis/AP Images, 79; Mary Altaffer/AP Images, 83; Steven Senne/AP Images, 88; Erin Edgerton/The Daily Progress/AP Images, 93; Matthew Hatcher/SOPA Images/Sipa USA/AP Images, 94

Editor: Marie Pearson
Designer: Becky Daum

Library of Congress Control Number: 2021951381
Publisher's Cataloging-in-Publication Data
Names: Deal, Heidi, author.
Title: Fighting covid-19 in the United States / by Heidi Deal
Description: Minneapolis, Minnesota : Abdo Publishing, 2023 | Series: Fighting covid-19 | Includes online resources and index.
Identifiers: ISBN 9781532197956 (lib. bdg.) | ISBN 9781098271602 (ebook)
Subjects: LCSH: COVID-19 (Disease)--Juvenile literature. | Social distancing (Public health)--Juvenile literature. | Communicable diseases--Vaccination--Juvenile literature. | Social hygiene--Juvenile literature. | Health--Public opinion--Juvenile literature. | Civilization, Modern--21st century--Juvenile literature. | United States--History--Juvenile literature.
Classification: DDC 614.592--dc23

CONTENTS

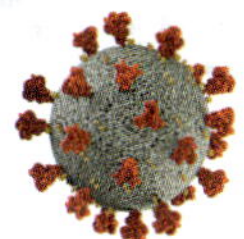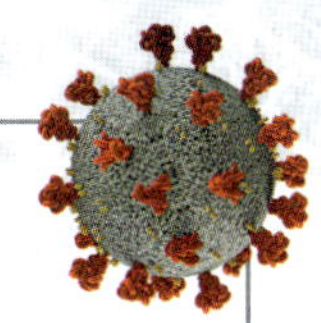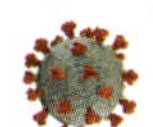

SEAL OF THE PRESIDENT OF THE UNITED STATES

PANDEMIC!

In January 2020, news began circulating about an unknown virus causing pneumonia. Reports of outbreaks were popping up all over China, and the disease began spreading around the world. Americans watched as the virus made its way to Italy, wreaking havoc on communities and locking down the country as citizens isolated themselves at home to avoid infection.

The director general of the World Health Organization (WHO) announced on March 11, 2020, that COVID-19 was officially a pandemic. The WHO is a United Nations organization that promotes global health by coordinating responses to international health emergencies, developing plans to improve overall health, and working to expand universal health coverage. On March 13, 2020, President Donald Trump declared a nationwide emergency and followed up three days later with a 15-day plan to combat the

US President Donald Trump declared a national emergency on March 13, 2020, due to the COVID-19 pandemic.

coronavirus outbreak.[1] Hundreds of new cases were being reported across the United States, hospitalizations were on the rise, and the number of deaths related to the new disease was growing. By March 15, the United States had reported more than 3,000 COVID-19 cases, and more than 60 people had already died from the disease.[2]

The 15-day plan advised Americans to stay home and avoid large groups. Schools shut down, sending students home for a planned two weeks. Non-essential businesses closed, and employees transitioned to working from home if they could. The eerie effects of the closures were seen in communities across the country. Freeways and beaches were empty. Airplanes were grounded. The normal hustle and bustle of daily life had essentially come to a stop as people hunkered down in their homes. In response to these guidelines, many states and local governments issued stay-at-home orders that required people to stay home except for essential trips, such as to get groceries or to get to an essential job, such as in a hospital or grocery store.

There were two primary goals of the 15-day plan. One goal was to slow the spread

> "Thick darkness has gathered over our squares, our streets, and our cities. It has taken over our lives, filling everything with a deafening silence and a distressing void that stops everything as it passes by; we feel it in the air. . . . We find ourselves afraid and lost."[3]
> —*Pope Francis, March 27, 2020*

of the new infectious disease by limiting close contact so people could not pass the virus to others. People practiced social distancing, which meant that they stayed at least six feet (1.8 m) away from people from other households. The other goal was to slow down the rate at which people were getting infected. This would lead to fewer people requiring hospitalization at the same time, and hospital staff would have the capacity to care for all of the patients.

WHAT IS COVID-19?

COVID-19 is short for coronavirus disease 2019. The virus that causes the infectious respiratory disease was first discovered in 2019 and is called SARS-CoV-2. The virus's name stands for severe acute respiratory syndrome coronavirus 2. It is from the same family as an earlier SARS coronavirus. Common symptoms of COVID-19 include fever, cough, loss of taste or smell, fatigue, sore throat, headache, and general body aches. The disease is considered serious when people have difficulty breathing, shortness of breath, chest pain, confusion, or loss of speech or mobility. Because of the respiratory nature of the disease, it resembles pneumonia and the flu.

The initial COVID-19 outbreak in the United States affected the elderly population the most. It was common to see news reports about nursing homes being devastated by the virus, causing many deaths in people over age 85. By March 2022, COVID-19 cases for those 85 and older accounted for

HOW DOES COVID-19 SPREAD?

COVID-19 is spread from one person to another when small airborne droplets from an infected person's mouth or nose are expelled when coughing, sneezing, speaking, or breathing. These droplets can stay airborne for up to three hours. People who come into contact with these airborne particles may become infected. Face masks reduce the amount of infected particles that escape a person's mouth and nose. They also help protect others from inhaling airborne particles.

almost 27 percent of the total deaths caused by COVID-19.
That same age group made up just 2 percent of the
total US population.[4] Children were the least affected
by the new virus, and even though they could carry and
pass it on to others, they showed very mild symptoms,
if any. But the illness was new and unknown, and to
prevent infecting others, it was important for everyone to
participate in the 15-day social distancing plan.

Health-care workers struggled with stress and burnout as
they treated a rising number of COVID-19 patients.

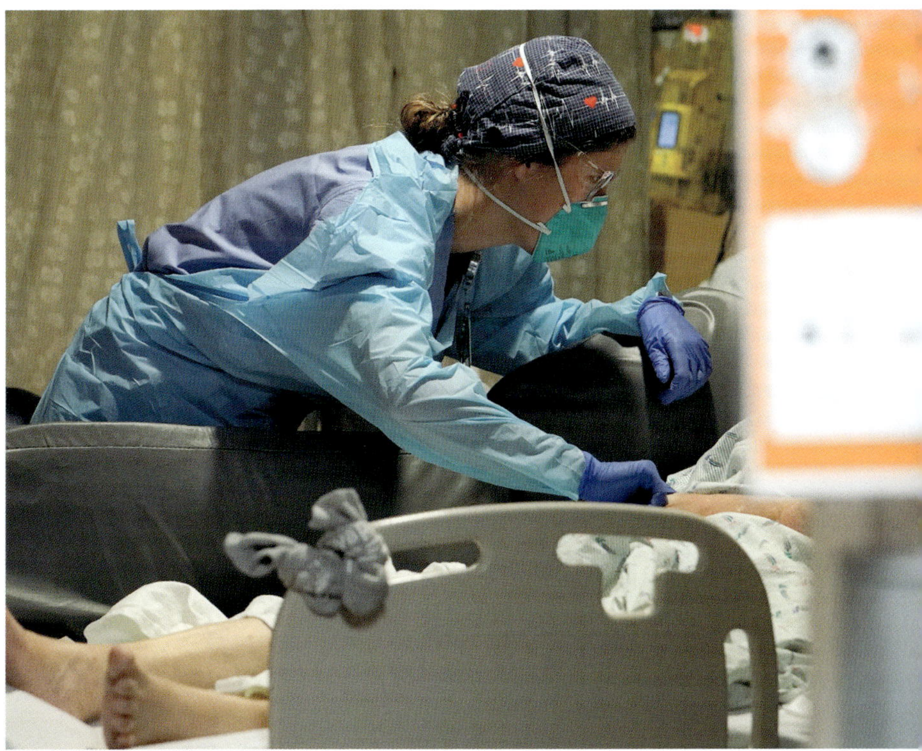

PUBLIC HEALTH EMERGENCY

On January 31, 2020, the WHO declared the coronavirus outbreak a public health emergency of international concern. The US Department of Health and Human Services (HHS) and the White House declared the outbreak a public health emergency the same day, announcing new travel policies. They went into effect just days later and restricted travel from various locations as a means to prevent the virus from being brought into the country.

In response to the COVID-19 outbreak, the US Centers for Disease Control and Prevention (CDC) and laboratories around the world developed diagnostic tests to identify whether a person's illness was caused by SARS-CoV-2. But testing didn't stop the virus. It only determined whether a person was infected.

Like tight-quartered nursing homes, cruise ships such as the *Diamond Princess* became hot spots for the spread of COVID-19. On February 1, 2020, a passenger tested positive in Hong Kong just days after disembarking the *Diamond Princess.* The cruise ship was notified of the infection, and all 3,711 passengers who had continued on the cruise were quarantined on the ship when it arrived in Japan. More than 700 people were infected, and seven died.[5] On March 14, the CDC issued a No Sail Order to all cruise ships. The Cruise Lines International Association obeyed the order by suspending cruise ship operations from ports in the United States.

There was no clear way to prevent or control COVID-19. Diseases caused by bacteria can be treated with medicines called antibiotics. But viral diseases, such as COVID-19, have few effective medicines. A person's immune system must fight off the infection. Early in the pandemic, the United States and other countries began taking many preventive measures to protect against infection. One of these solutions was the use of face masks. It became commonplace for people to wear face masks anytime they went into public places such as grocery stores or gas stations. The fear of this new disease led to a shortage of medical-grade masks. These are most commonly used in hospitals by medical professionals. The surge of regular people seeking them for everyday use caused the prices to go up, and manufacturers couldn't produce them quickly enough.

Hand sanitizer was also in high demand. One way to prevent infection is to keep hands clean. Handwashing is the most effective way to do this, but hand sanitizer allowed people to quickly clean their hands on the go. Bottles of hand sanitizer could be found in many cars, purses, and households so people could disinfect their hands after touching something that someone else had touched before them. According to the *Wall Street Journal*, hand sanitizer sales jumped 600 percent in 2020.[6]

Like face masks, hand sanitizer became hard to find. Stores couldn't keep their shelves stocked, and they placed limits on the amount each person could purchase. The demand was so high that breweries and distilleries across the country shut down production of beer, gin, and whiskey. They began using their equipment to manufacture alcohol-based hand sanitizer to distribute to local communities, often for free.

There were a variety of responses from government officials and health experts, and the fight against the disease changed as they learned more about the virus. Some thought the virus would fizzle out in a few months, but it continued to spread through US communities and around the world, and temporary preventive measures soon became the new normal.

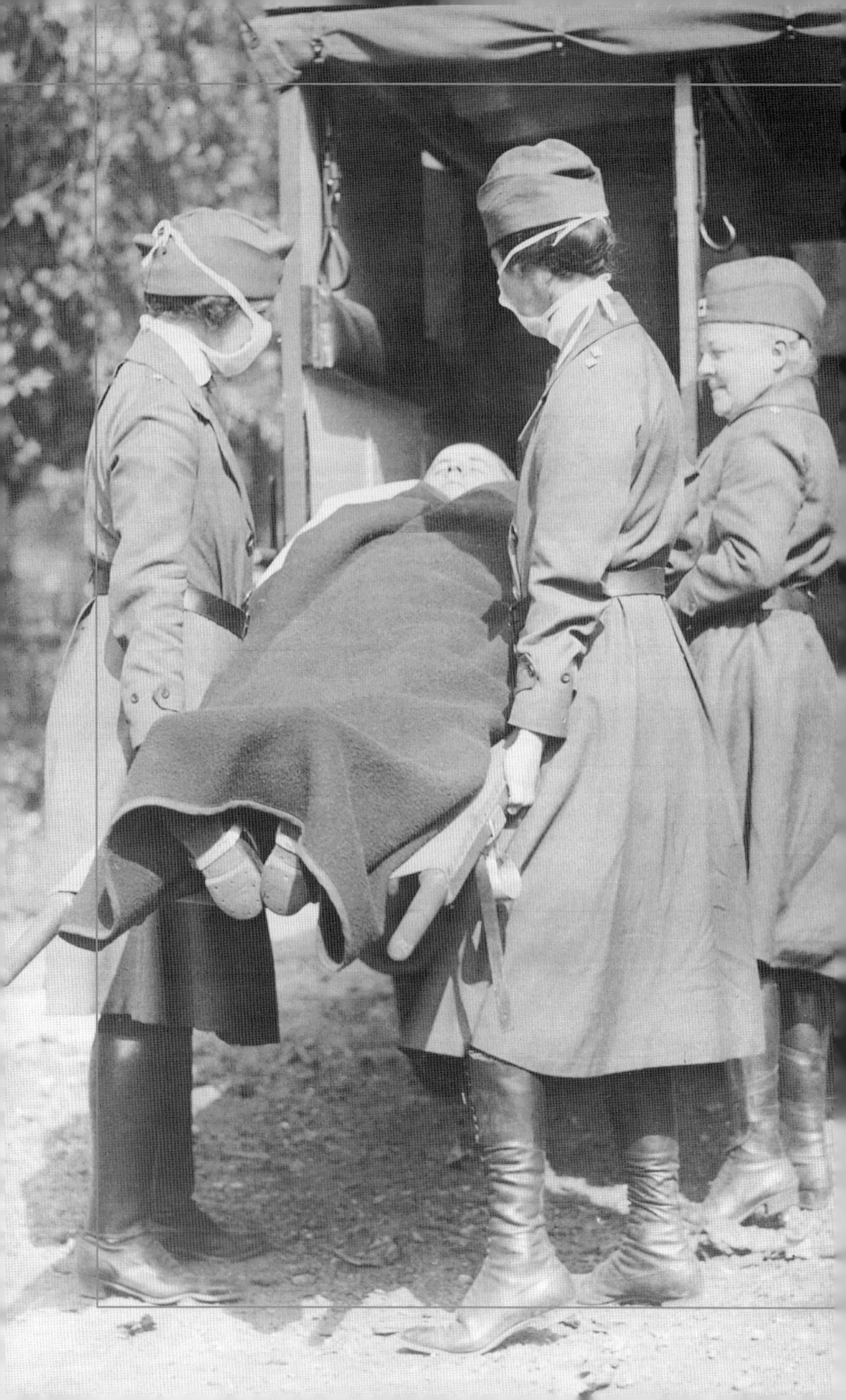

OUTBREAKS PAST AND PRESENT

COVID-19 was not the first pandemic in the United States. The disease and the ways people fight it are most commonly compared to the flu pandemic that began in 1918. The 1918 flu, a type of influenza, was the most devastating pandemic in recent history. This H1N1 virus may have originated in Kansas. It first affected soldiers during World War I (1914–1918) and spread quickly across the globe, infecting approximately 500 million people and killing an estimated 50 million people. In the United States, there were approximately 675,000 deaths.[1]

People who contracted the 1918 flu suffered from severe pneumonia. The lungs would fill with bodily fluids, depriving the body of oxygen and drowning the infected person. The 1918 flu was especially deadly for children younger than age five, and the death rate

Health-care workers were stretched thin during the 1918 flu pandemic.

was greatest for people ages 15 to 40. Healthy people frequently succumbed to the 1918 flu, making it especially concerning. There was no vaccine for the disease during the 1918 flu outbreak, so treatment and prevention relied heavily on isolation, hygiene, and the use of disinfectants.

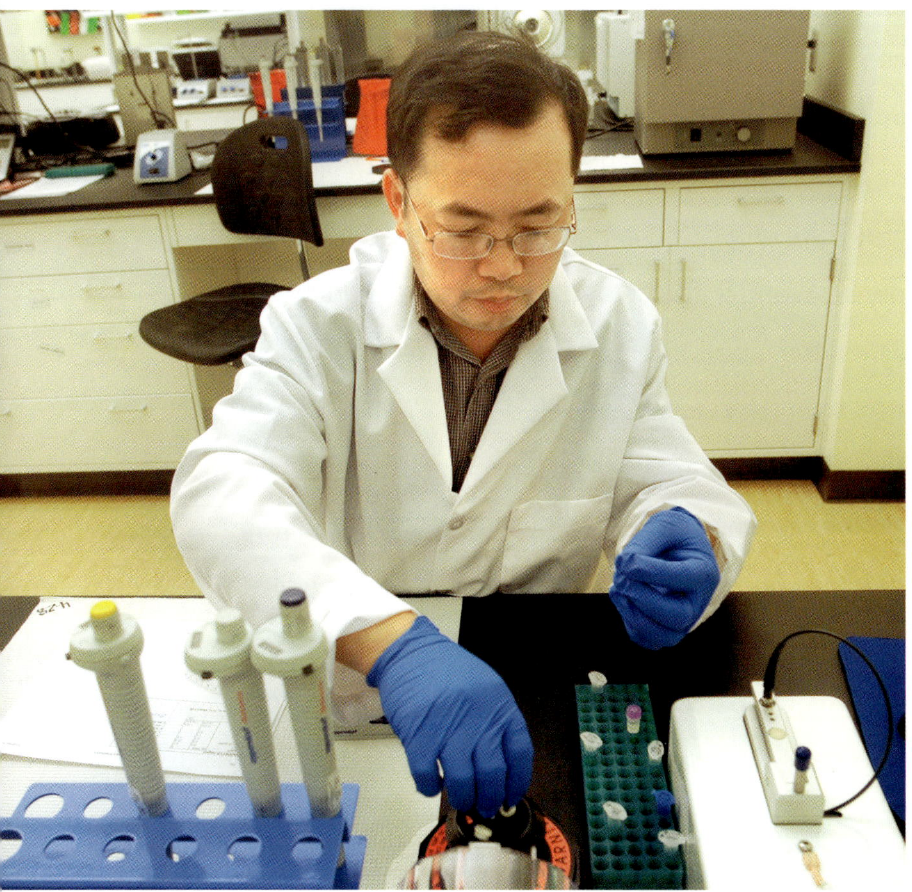

During the swine flu pandemic in 2009, the CDC reserved the most accurate tests for people who were hospitalized or had weak immune systems.

There have been several infectious disease epidemics throughout US history besides the 1918 flu. A new H1N1 variant that caused the swine flu emerged in the United States in the spring of 2009 and spread quickly across the nation and the world. There were approximately 60 million cases of H1N1 illnesses and more than 12,000 deaths in the United States.[2] Although the disease was similar to the seasonal flu, existing vaccines offered little protection from the new strain, and it took nearly seven months to develop a new vaccine.

People younger than age 65, especially children and young adults, accounted for the majority of the deaths. Respiratory complications caused the most deaths during the H1N1 outbreak. The WHO declared an end to the pandemic in 2010, but the H1N1 virus continues to circulate as a seasonal flu virus.

EARLY DAYS OF COVID-19

Even though there have been past pandemics, people were largely unprepared for COVID-19. In December 2019, patients in Wuhan, China, began suffering from symptoms that included fever and difficulty breathing. The illness initially presented like the flu or pneumonia.

Doctors in China worked to find an accurate diagnosis for their patients.

On December 27, 2019, a Chinese lab identified the illness as a coronavirus, much like the severe acute respiratory syndrome (SARS) virus of 2002. SARS infected more than 8,000 people globally, causing nearly 800 deaths between November 2002 and July 2003. That virus ran its course, and no new cases have been reported since 2004.[3]

The lab alerted health authorities about the discovery of the new virus, but the information was initially kept from the public. By December 30, 2019, Chinese doctors were sharing the news with colleagues, warning about the unknown illness, and this information soon made its way across social media. Dr. Li Wenliang shared a lab report with information about the new SARS-like virus. Li and several others were detained by police for supposedly spreading rumors and

> "If we can't be a whistleblower like Li Wenliang, then let us at least be someone who hears that whistle."[4]
>
> *—Yan Lianke, professor, Hong Kong University of Science and Technology*

misinformation and were forced to sign an agreement
to remain quiet or face legal troubles. Just weeks later, Li
died at the age of 33 after contracting COVID-19.

ORIGIN OF COVID-19

Early cases of the
virus were linked to
the Huanan Seafood
Wholesale Market in
Wuhan, so officials
closed down the market.
This type of facility was
known as a wet market.
More than 1,000 vendors
sold a variety of goods
there, including fish,
meat, produce, other
perishables, and live
animals. The market is
considered to be the center of the COVID-19 outbreak.
Nearly two-thirds of the original 41 people hospitalized
with the pneumonia-like symptoms had been in contact
with the market.[5]

But the origin of the virus remained in question. The first patient presented symptoms on December 1, 2019, and had no connection to the market, leading researchers to believe that the virus may have originated elsewhere, weeks earlier than what was being reported. Where and when exactly were still unknown.

A few theories circulated about the origin of the new coronavirus. Some people believed that it originated in wild bats and spread to other wild animals before a human came in contact with one of the infected animals at a wet market. Other people thought it was possible that a scientist in a lab who was working with experimental bat viruses became infected and spread the disease to other humans.

After the closure of the Wuhan market on January 1, 2020, officials collected and tested 585 environmental samples from the market. Thirty-three of those samples were

BATS AND CORONAVIRUSES

Reports circulated around the globe that bats were the source of the COVID-19 outbreak. This was never officially confirmed, and there is no evidence that bats were the cause of the new coronavirus. Bats do carry coronaviruses, but scientists do not think they show any symptoms. Cats and camels are other coronavirus carriers.

positive for SARS-CoV-2.[6] This indicated that it was highly likely that infection could have occurred there, or in any other wet market where infected live animals were being sold. The exact origin of infection will likely remain a mystery.

EARLY RESPONSE

When word of the mysterious new virus reached the United States, it became a common topic of discussion. People were concerned but not panicked. By January 3, the Chinese Center for Disease Control and Prevention had fully identified the virus and reported the outbreak to the WHO. However, the Chinese government continued to keep it quiet from the general public and media, even going so far as ordering hospitals and labs to destroy patient samples.

Evidence that the virus was spreading came on January 13, 2020, when the first case of COVID-19 was confirmed in Thailand, and Japan followed with a confirmed case on January 15. In the United States, major airports in Los Angeles, California; San Francisco, California; and New York City began screening for the new virus on January 17, focusing primarily on passengers

In April 2020, the Hawaii National Guard began to screen for COVID-19 by taking the temperature of passengers flying in to and out of the state.

traveling internationally from Wuhan. The CDC focused on contact tracing efforts. Initial screening included questioning passengers about whether they had related symptoms such as fever, cough, or difficulty breathing.

The WHO confirmed human-to-human spread on January 22, just days after the first case of COVID-19 was identified in the United States. This confirmed that the virus was not limited to infection from an animal to a person. When a virus can be transmitted among people, the disease has the ability to spread much more quickly and affect far more people.

On January 29, the White House established a Coronavirus Task Force to monitor the outbreak and take action to manage and contain the spread of the virus. The Trump administration followed the WHO by declaring a public health emergency on January 31. It placed travel restrictions on people coming from Wuhan. The travel restrictions faced controversy early on. Even the director general of the WHO stated that travel restrictions increased fear and weren't beneficial to public health. However, countries all over the world were imposing travel restrictions, and they would continue to do so more than a year into the pandemic.

Later, the controversy shifted, and President Trump was criticized for not enacting travel restrictions sooner. The coronavirus pandemic was fluid and evolving.

People criticized the early response as being too much too soon, but it was later viewed as too

PUBLIC HEALTH EMERGENCIES OF THE PAST

The WHO has declared global public health emergencies only six times since 2007, reserving them for extraordinary events that pose a global health risk. The public health emergencies of international concern were for the 2009 H1N1 influenza, Ebola in 2013 to 2015 and 2018 to 2020, poliomyelitis in 2014, Zika in 2016, and COVID-19 in 2020.

little too late. The United States and the world were not prepared for an outbreak of this magnitude. Additionally, the pandemic was emerging amid Trump's impeachment trial, though he was acquitted by the US Senate on February 5, 2020. There was extreme polarization between Democrats and Republicans, and the way the coronavirus outbreak was handled came under fire later for being too politicized. The public was at times confused about the messages they received from different parts of the government. Even after HHS declared a public health emergency, Democratic House Speaker Nancy Pelosi took to the streets of San Francisco's Chinatown District in early February, encouraging people to visit, saying precautions were being taken and it was safe to continue visiting despite the growing pandemic.

Testing was a key component to the early response. The production and distribution of reliable tests was a slow-moving process, but by March 7, more than 1,000 cases had been diagnosed and 27 deaths had been attributed to COVID-19 in the United States. As diagnostic tests became more readily available, the number of cases climbed rapidly. The death toll passed 100 on March 16, and by April 1, reported cases reached more than 223,000

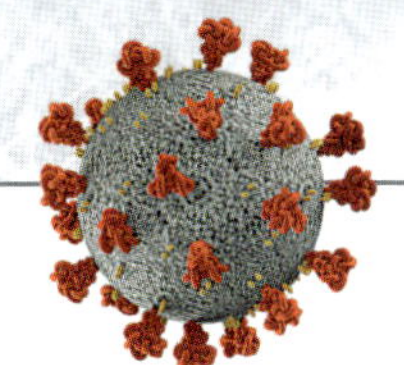

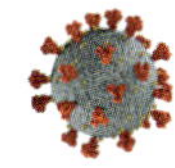

DAILY US DEATHS IN MARCH 2020[7]

In March 2020, the rising number of COVID-19 cases and deaths prompted health and government officials to take action. As hospitals filled with sick and dying patients, the health-care system became strained. On March 19, California was first in the country to issue a statewide stay-at-home order. Other states followed throughout the rest of the month and into April. Under these orders, public gatherings were not allowed. People could not eat at restaurants, work out at gyms, or watch movies in theaters. People who could work from home did so, while others couldn't work at all or even lost their jobs because of temporary lockdowns. Some businesses and activities, however, were deemed essential. People could get groceries at the grocery store, pick up medications at the pharmacy, and go to the hospital if they needed care. People who worked for these essential businesses often still had to go to work. The goal of the lockdowns was to reduce COVID-19 infections and deaths and relieve health-care workers to give them more time to understand how to treat and prevent the virus.

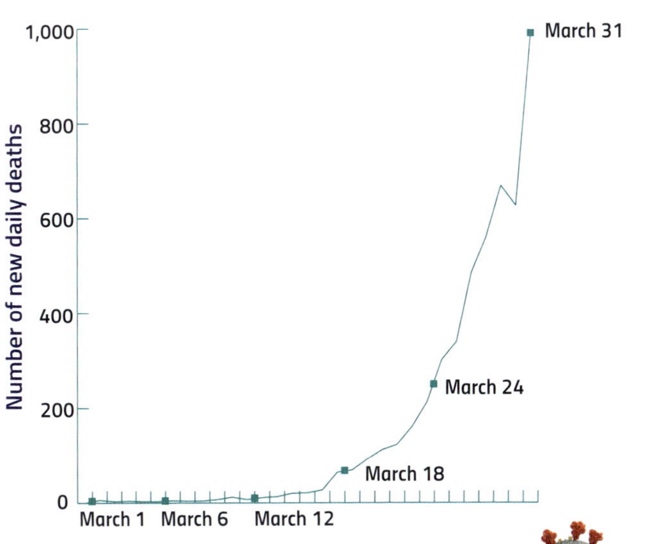

Some people tried to help ease the ventilator shortage by building simple ventilators for hospitals.

with 5,337 deaths. Less than one month later, the number of cases soared to more than one million. COVID-19 deaths passed 54,000.[8]

During the spring of 2020, there was a severe lack of adequate personal protective equipment (PPE) and ventilators. A ventilator is a medical device that moves air into a patient's lungs, which helps the patient breathe. Due to consumer demand, hospitals faced a shortage of necessary supplies such as masks and gowns to protect workers as they treated patients. President Trump invoked the Defense Production Act in April to secure contracts with companies to make ventilators and stop the export of PPE to other countries. Shortly after, Trump began contracting with companies to increase production of face masks. New supplies slowly made their way to health-care workers who desperately needed them, but shortages lasted well into the summer of 2020. Once producers were able to provide these ventilators, though, treatment for the virus was starting to evolve and doctors were relying less on the machines. This led to an excess of ventilators in the federal stockpile.

HOT SPOTS

Many factors contributed to the increase of COVID-19 cases. Early in the pandemic, the cities and locations that were hot spots became so because of dense populations. They also had more people with chronic health issues such as diabetes, obesity, high blood pressure, and asthma. New York City, the most densely populated US city, was a hot spot in the spring of 2020.

WHO'S IN CHARGE?

Many people worked together behind the scenes in a variety of roles during the fight against COVID-19. Some worked to find treatments for the virus, and others were working to develop procedures to help communities across the country prevent infection. Entire organizations also played key roles.

Dr. Tedros Adhanom Ghebreyesus had served as Ethiopia's minister of health from 2005 to 2012 and as minister of foreign affairs from 2012 to 2016 before being elected as the WHO's director general in 2017. He was serving in this position when COVID-19 emerged. Throughout the pandemic he met with world leaders and emphasized the importance of wealthy nations supporting developing countries during the crisis.

The WHO's China office received notification of the unknown illnesses on December 31, 2019. The organization later announced a name for the disease,

Dr. Tedros Adhanom Ghebreyesus led the WHO during the COVID-19 pandemic.

calling it COVID-19. The WHO declared the outbreak a pandemic on March 11, 2020, raising the level of the health emergency and urging communities to take additional precautions to curb the spread of the virus.

The WHO's recommendations laid the groundwork for how state and federal governments addressed the COVID-19 response throughout the United States. The WHO developed several strategy reports to outline goals and procedures related to COVID-19. The Strategic Preparedness and Response Plan (SPRP) from April 2020 stated that the overall goal was to slow down transmission and reduce mortality. Objectives included encouraging community members to practice individual protection measures such as handwashing, avoiding touching their faces, and practicing social distancing. It also emphasized finding, testing, and isolating patients with COVID-19, providing proper care, and quarantining others who may have come in contact with the infected individuals. The WHO suggested reducing community transmission by limiting gatherings, closing schools and non-essential businesses, and reducing public transportation. Many communities across the United States followed its recommendations.

As time went by, the WHO continued to update its reports and add to them as needed in response to the evolving pandemic. By May 2021, the SPRP report included ten areas of focus such as surveillance and contact tracing, supervision of mass gatherings and points of entry, infection prevention and control, laboratories and diagnostics, and therapeutics and vaccination. The reports provided detailed recommendations and information to support their reasoning.

In the beginning of the pandemic, the WHO provided global guidance and recommendations for managing the outbreak. In the United States, federal agencies used the WHO's guidance to develop national policies and recommendations. There were mixed messages in the beginning on masks, social interaction, and travel. However, once the pandemic was well underway and the virus was better understood, the general recommendations became more consistent. Americans were advised to wear masks, practice social distancing, wash their hands often, cover their mouths and noses when coughing or sneezing, isolate themselves from others when ill or after receiving a positive COVID-19 test, and get vaccinated. Enforcement of the policies and recommendations fell on local communities.

THE CDC

The CDC is a national organization dedicated to protecting the health of the US public and responding to disease threats as they arise. As a health protection agency, it conducts essential scientific research and provides information to the public regarding all health and safety threats, diseases, and disabilities. The CDC addresses major health issues affecting Americans, provides critical leadership and training to the public health workforce, and uses advanced technology to work toward disease prevention. The CDC website provides useful information and resources such as updates on

Dr. Anthony Fauci of the National Institute of Allergy and Infectious Diseases, *left*, and Dr. Rochelle P. Walensky of the CDC, *right*, testified before a US Senate committee about the COVID-19 response.

recent infectious outbreaks, emergency preparedness, general health guidance and disease prevention, vaccine descriptions, and recommendations for travelers.

Robert R. Redfield served as director of the CDC at the start of the pandemic and into 2021. Then, in 2021, President Joe Biden appointed Rochelle P. Walensky as director. Throughout the pandemic, the CDC provided extensive coverage of the spread of the virus, rates of infection and death, and the development of testing and vaccines. The CDC was one of the primary sources of guidance for managing risk and prevention during the pandemic. It also developed Clara, an interactive online

The FDA headquarters are in Maryland.

coronavirus symptom checker that chatted virtually with users about symptoms, risk factors, and management of infection at home if the user was sick.

THE FDA

The US Food and Drug Administration (FDA) partnered with the US government, the CDC, and other agencies to address public health during the pandemic. Its primary focus was facilitating the development of tests, vaccines, medications, and medical devices to fight COVID-19. The FDA is responsible for reviewing and approving these products and determining if they are fit to be used by the public. For example, after the CDC developed a diagnostic test for COVID-19, it submitted the test to the FDA for approval before producing and distributing it.

All tests and vaccines developed during the pandemic were approved by the FDA before use. Most of these products were initially approved under emergency use authorization (EUA), meaning the products had not been fully reviewed and approved but were acceptable to use if there were no available alternatives. Medications that were developed to fight COVID-19 were also reviewed by the FDA and received EUA or full approval.

Stephen M. Hahn was FDA commissioner when the pandemic started. In 2021, President Biden nominated Robert M. Califf for the position. Congress approved Califf as the new commissioner in February 2022.

DEPARTMENT OF HEALTH AND HUMAN SERVICES

HHS is an executive branch department of the US government that provides services to protect the health of the American public. HHS works closely with the CDC and the FDA to provide guidance to the government and Americans. Throughout the pandemic, the HHS website maintained extensive information and resources for the public regarding tests, vaccines, relief funds, prevention, mental health, telehealth, and general education about the virus. Alex Azar was the secretary of HHS when the pandemic hit. In March 2021, Congress approved President Biden's nominee, Xavier Becerra, as the new secretary.

The FDA and the CDC both operate under HHS. The HHS COVID-19 public education campaign, We Can Do This, was developed to increase vaccine confidence and reinforce general prevention strategies, such as social distancing and mask wearing. This site was regularly updated as recommendations and guidance evolved. We Can Do This included video and social media ads encouraging various demographic groups to get vaccinated, including superhero-themed posters telling pediatric patients five and older to get their "superpower."[2]

CONGRESS

The US Congress consists of two chambers: the Senate and the House of Representatives. In 2020, as the pandemic hit, Republicans were in control of the Senate, and Mitch McConnell served as majority leader.

Nancy Pelosi, *left*, and Mitch McConnell, *right*, were two key figures in Congress during the pandemic.

Democrats controlled the House, and Nancy Pelosi served as speaker. The US Congress writes legislation and votes on it. If both the House and Senate pass legislation, it is sent to the president to sign into law. The president can choose to veto, or reject, the legislation. However, Congress can override that veto if at least two-thirds of each chamber vote in favor of it.

Congress passed many pieces of legislation relating to COVID-19. One of the key pieces of legislation it passed was the Coronavirus Aid, Relief, and Economic Security (CARES) Act, which was signed into law on March 27, 2020. The act included many responses to the pandemic, including stimulus payments and extra unemployment payments to support individuals during times of job loss and business closure and to encourage them to spend money to keep the economy afloat. Based on income, people were eligible to receive up to $1,200, plus $500 for each child. Also, unemployed Americans were eligible to receive $600 per week added to their regular unemployment income.[3] The act also provided aid to community and private health systems, as well as forgivable loans to help small businesses that were temporarily shut down.

PRESIDENT DONALD TRUMP

When COVID-19 first emerged, President Trump was in office. He was the voice of the nation as the virus began spreading through the country. Following WHO and CDC guidance, his administration began working with officials to determine the best course of action for the United States. To manage and contain the new coronavirus, President Trump created the White House Coronavirus Task Force. The task force monitored the situation as it evolved. It provided updates on spread, prevention, and testing, as well as guidance on policies and reopening protocols. The Trump administration also created Operation Warp Speed (OWS), an effort to develop and distribute an effective vaccine within an accelerated time frame. This program allowed vaccine companies to combine clinical trial phases, and by mid-December 2020, two of the resulting vaccines received EUA from the FDA, and Americans began receiving the shots.

The president and his administration took many additional steps to ensure the well-being of the nation, such as imposing early travel restrictions and screening protocols. The administration also used executive orders to expand funding for the development of testing and the production of medical supplies. And it worked with Congress to pass the CARES Act to get stimulus payments to the American people. The first round of stimulus checks

President Biden signed the American Rescue Plan into law on March 12, 2021.

was sent out in April 2020. President Trump approved legislation passed by Congress to send a second round of payments that went to eligible Americans beginning in December 2020.

Some criticized President Trump for minimizing the severity of the virus in the early days of the outbreak. On February 27, 2020, he stated, "It's going to disappear. One day—it's like a miracle—it will disappear."[4] However, little was known about the virus, and the outbreak of COVID-19 was a global event that changed and evolved on a daily basis. Worldwide, the response to the new virus was poorly handled. Scientists had been predicting an imminent pandemic for years. But the US government, like many others around the world, had done little to prepare. Governments were not ready for the virus to spread as widely and as quickly as it did.

PRESIDENT JOE BIDEN

President Biden took office in January 2021, a year after the pandemic began. In March, he signed into law the American Rescue Plan, which offered more stimulus payments. His administration also implemented a six-pronged national strategy called the Path Out of the Pandemic to combat COVID-19. It included vaccinating the unvaccinated, protecting the vaccinated with additional booster shots, keeping schools open safely, increasing testing and requiring masks, improving care for people infected with the virus, and protecting the recovery of the economy.

The Path Out of the Pandemic provided funding for school districts, expanded production of tests, and supported small businesses impacted by the pandemic with long-term, low-cost loans. It also deployed additional health-care professionals to support medical facilities experiencing a surge in COVID-19 patients. The Biden administration's plan included mask and vaccine mandates. This addition was different from Biden's original stance. In December 2020, he assured the American people that vaccines would not be made mandatory and masks would be encouraged but never forced.

Like Trump, President Biden was also criticized for his pandemic management. Seema Lakdawala, a virologist at the University of Pittsburgh, said, "I do think that there may have been an overemphasis on vaccination as being the easy way to solve this at the cost of testing and other mitigation strategies that we could have continued to do to reduce some of the burden that we've seen."[5] But as was the case under Trump, the pandemic remained a constantly changing situation.

DR. ANTHONY FAUCI

Dr. Anthony Fauci is an immunologist. During the pandemic he served as the director of the National Institute of Allergy and Infectious Diseases, one of the branches of the National Institutes of Health (NIH). Fauci has acted as an adviser to every president from Ronald

Reagan to Biden. Starting in 2020, Fauci served as one of the leaders of the White House Coronavirus Task Force and was often the face of the updates regarding the COVID-19 pandemic. Fauci provided guidance to the American public.

Fauci faced accusations from some, including Senator Rand Paul, that he had played a role in starting the pandemic and was responsible for millions of deaths. These claims were not supported by evidence, but some people sent Fauci death threats because of the claims. Senator Mitt Romney said to Fauci, "You are being made subject to the political whims of various political individuals. And that comes at a high cost, which unfortunately, I fear will lead some to not want to participate in helping our government."[6]

Fauci was an experienced immunologist who was in charge of the responses to past epidemics including HIV/AIDS and Ebola. He was a significant voice during the COVID-19 pandemic, delivering the federal government's recommendations for prevention and policies to the American people and offering regular updates regarding the state of the outbreak, the virus, and additional mutations as the pandemic evolved.

STATE GOVERNMENTS

In April 2020, President Trump announced that states should have the primary responsibility of containing the outbreak within their communities.

This gave state and local officials the ability to adjust policies for containment and prevention to better accommodate their unique needs. While the federal government suggested following recommendations by the CDC, it was up to individual states to decide on policies for social distancing, masking, traveling, testing requirements, and stay-at-home orders.

States varied in their responses to the pandemic. Disagreements often reflected partisan values, again bringing politicization to the outbreak. Republican-controlled state restrictions and policies differed from those in Democrat-controlled states, with Democrats favoring stricter policies than Republicans. States with Republican governors, such as Florida and Texas, favored open businesses and fewer mandates for masks and vaccines, while states such as California and Oregon with Democratic governors favored longer shutdowns, stricter mask guidelines, and mandatory vaccination. One study determined that the risk of dying from COVID-19 in states with Republican governors was 1.8 times higher than in states with Democratic governors.[9]

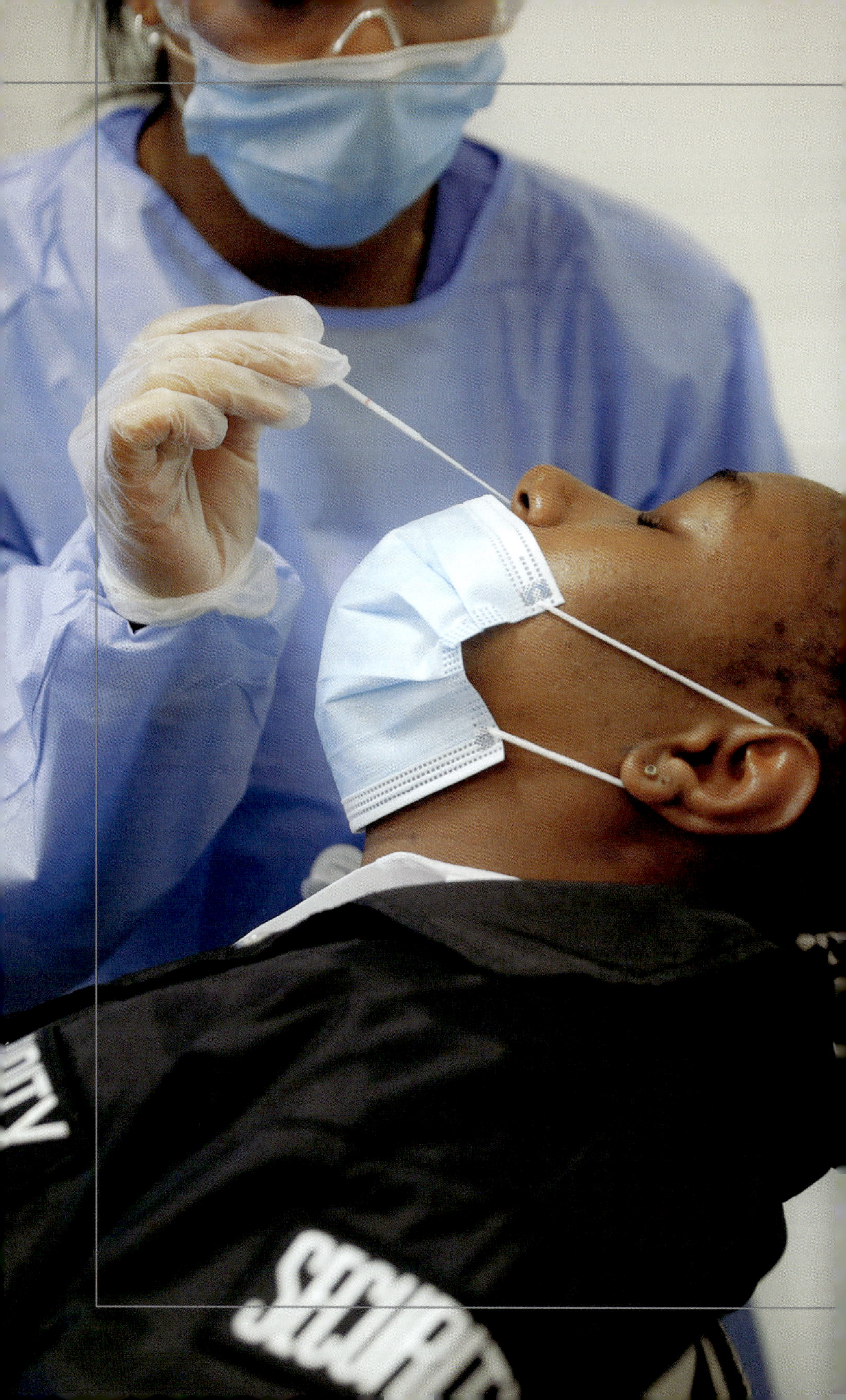

TESTING, TESTING

The fight against COVID-19 relied heavily on testing. Testing helped identify who was infected with the virus, and it allowed researchers to track the number of cases. By February 3, 2020, the CDC submitted to the FDA a diagnostic test for use by health professionals. At that point, only three cases had been confirmed in the United States. The first 200 test kits were distributed to labs the next day on February 4.[1] Early in the pandemic, tests were not readily available. Over time, several tests were developed and manufactured, and they were often free of charge to the public.

A viral polymerase chain reaction (PCR) test was the most common form of testing used during the pandemic to detect a current infection. In this test, a swab was used to collect mucus samples, usually from the nose but sometimes from the mouth. This test was recommended for people who had symptoms

COVID-19 tests often required collecting a mucus sample with a nasal swab.

of COVID-19 and those who had been in contact with infected people. PCR tests were designed to identify viral RNA. Tests were sent to labs for analysis. Early on, it could take several days to receive results, though later in the pandemic the results were generally available within 48 hours.[2] In May 2020, the FDA approved a rapid antigen test similar to the PCR, allowing for quicker results, but these tended to be less accurate in their early days. Rapid antigen tests also use swabs, but unlike PCR tests, antigen tests detect proteins on the surface of the virus to identify infection.

Drive-through testing sites popped up across the country at places such as baseball stadiums, parking lots, convention centers, and pharmacies. Dodger Stadium, home of baseball's Los Angeles Dodgers, had the capacity to test up to 6,000 people every day.[3] People across the country flocked to testing sites, sometimes leading to hours-long waits. Samples were collected by volunteers and health-care workers in protective gear who swabbed noses through partly opened windows and sent the swabs to labs.

During the course of the pandemic, viral testing became commonplace. Some people had to get tested and show they were free of infection in order to work. People would also get tested before or after travel and before or after large gatherings with family or friends. Because of the body's ability to create natural antibodies when exposed to the virus, the CDC said that people who tested positive for the virus didn't need to get retested for the next three months if they didn't have any symptoms.

TYPES OF COVID-19 TESTS

Early in the pandemic, COVID-19 tests were available only at testing sites such as doctors' offices, pharmacies, and designated testing locations. The first available tests for the general public used swabs inserted in the nose. Later, researchers developed tests that could detect the virus in saliva. The spit tests were a welcome alternative for people who didn't like the nasal swab. By the end of 2021, a variety of over-the-counter self-testing options were available at most drug stores.

ANTIBODY TESTS

The antibody test was an additional kind of test that scientists developed. When the body's immune system encounters a new infection, it generates proteins called antibodies. Antibodies recognize invading bacteria and viruses, attach to them, and destroy them. They are an important way the immune system fights disease.

Antibody tests for COVID-19 are designed to detect the antibodies that the body creates against the SARS-CoV-2 virus. These tests are used to detect past infections rather than present ones, because it can take the body a few weeks to develop antibodies. They require blood to be drawn and tested by a health-care professional.

NATURAL ANTIBODIES

Testing for antibodies was a way to determine if someone had been previously infected by COVID-19. Because the virus was new, there was no way of knowing how long the antibodies from a natural infection would last for COVID-19. Scientists' estimates ranged from three months to five years.[4] In comparison, a study in 2008 found survivors of the 1918 flu still had significant antibodies for the virus in their blood. Antibodies help protect people from disease, but reinfection is still possible.

CONTACT TRACING

Contact tracing was one key way to slowing the

spread of COVID-19. When someone tested positive for the virus, friends and family who may have come in contact with the infected individual were notified about the exposure. Contacts were advised to get tested, monitor symptoms, wear masks, and minimize contact with others for 14 days from the date of exposure.

With COVID-19, contact tracers interviewed infected patients to learn who may have been exposed. Those people were notified and interviewed. Some states, such as California, implemented digital contact tracing tools allowing people to opt in to a program that would alert them if they had come in contact with another person who tested positive for COVID-19. Only people who opted in to the program and shared their phone information could be identified through this digital tool, and Bluetooth technology on cell phones identified when participants crossed paths.

PROBLEMS WITH TESTING

Across the United States, tests were being used to detect the virus, but because the virus was new, it took time to produce and distribute tests. Tests that were being developed by CDC-approved labs faced complications.

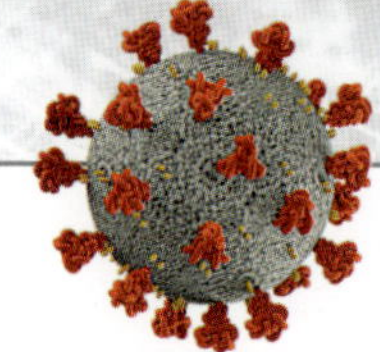
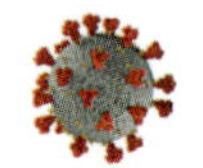

COVID-19 TESTING BY MONTH[5]

Testing in the United States got off to a slow start, complicated by a faulty CDC test. Testing was a critical piece to understanding where the virus was spreading and identifying who was infected so that measures could be taken to prevent further spread. The CDC began tracking the number of tests performed daily beginning on March 1, 2020, with about 300 tests.[6] As more kits became available, testing grew daily, sometimes by the thousands. The highest points of testing were during late 2020 into early 2021, with test numbers topping two million new tests per day.[7]

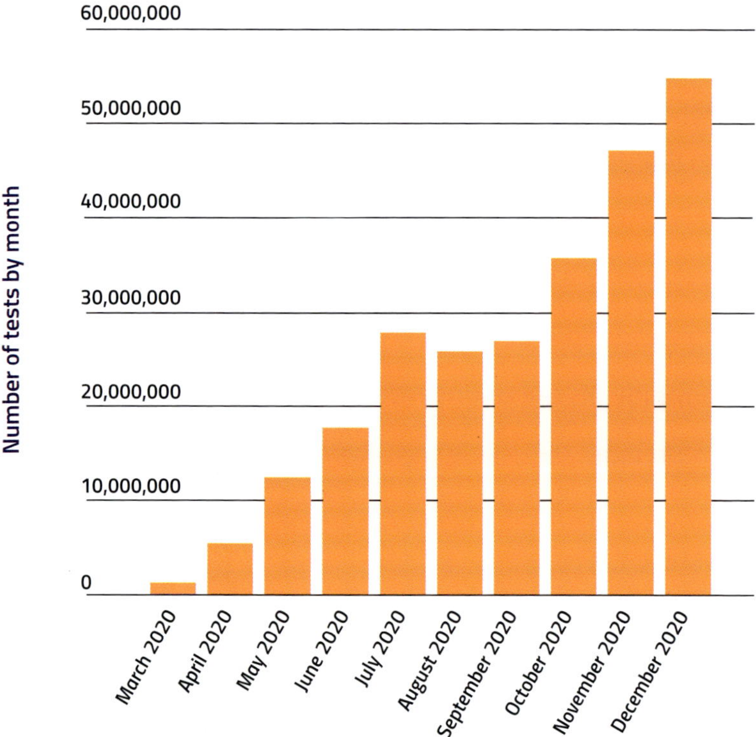

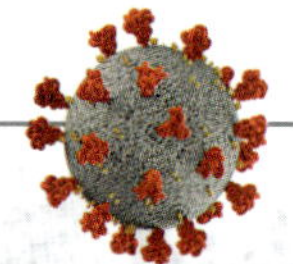

In February 2020, tests were proven to fail up to 33 percent of the time, causing a question of reliability.[8] At the same time, government regulations prevented scientists at academic, hospital, and public health labs from working on their own tests, even though some had already begun the research. The government stopped production to correct the test kit issues and eventually improved the CDC tests. The FDA later relaxed its policy to allow additional certified laboratories to contribute because of the high demand for testing. Then, in April 2020, unapproved antibody tests manufactured in China made their way to Colorado, California, Maryland, and North Carolina. The tests were reported to be unreliable, producing false results, both negative and positive.

—Keith Jerome, head of virology at the University of Washington, on March 5, 2020

Throughout the pandemic, there were issues with availability, quality, and reliability of tests. Through most of February 2020, there were fewer than ten tests per day. It wasn't until March that the testing really got underway. By March 15, thousands of tests were being processed daily, and by the end of 2020 more than one million tests were reported daily, sometimes climbing to more than two million.[10] The low number of tests early in the pandemic was problematic because researchers looking at disease transmission in New York City estimated that more than half of the people spreading COVID-19 had no symptoms or had not yet developed symptoms. Without testing, people could not know they were contagious and continued to spread the disease.

In California, a testing facility came under scrutiny. In October 2020, whistleblowers reported that lab techs were sleeping on the job, that test swabs were being left in unsanitary locations leading to possible contamination, and that the staff lacked proper training. Health inspectors labeled the lab a severe threat to the health and safety of recipients. Only 40 percent of tests were processed within 24 hours, which was one of the lowest rates in the state.[11] Despite the challenges faced by COVID-19 testing,

At some points during the pandemic, test shortages meant people who had been exposed to COVID-19 and were not showing symptoms could not get tested, even though they may have been infected.

the FDA and the CDC stood by the overall accuracy of testing, stating that it played an effective role in reducing the spread of the virus. It helped people know when they had to stay at home and limit contact with others to avoid spreading the disease.

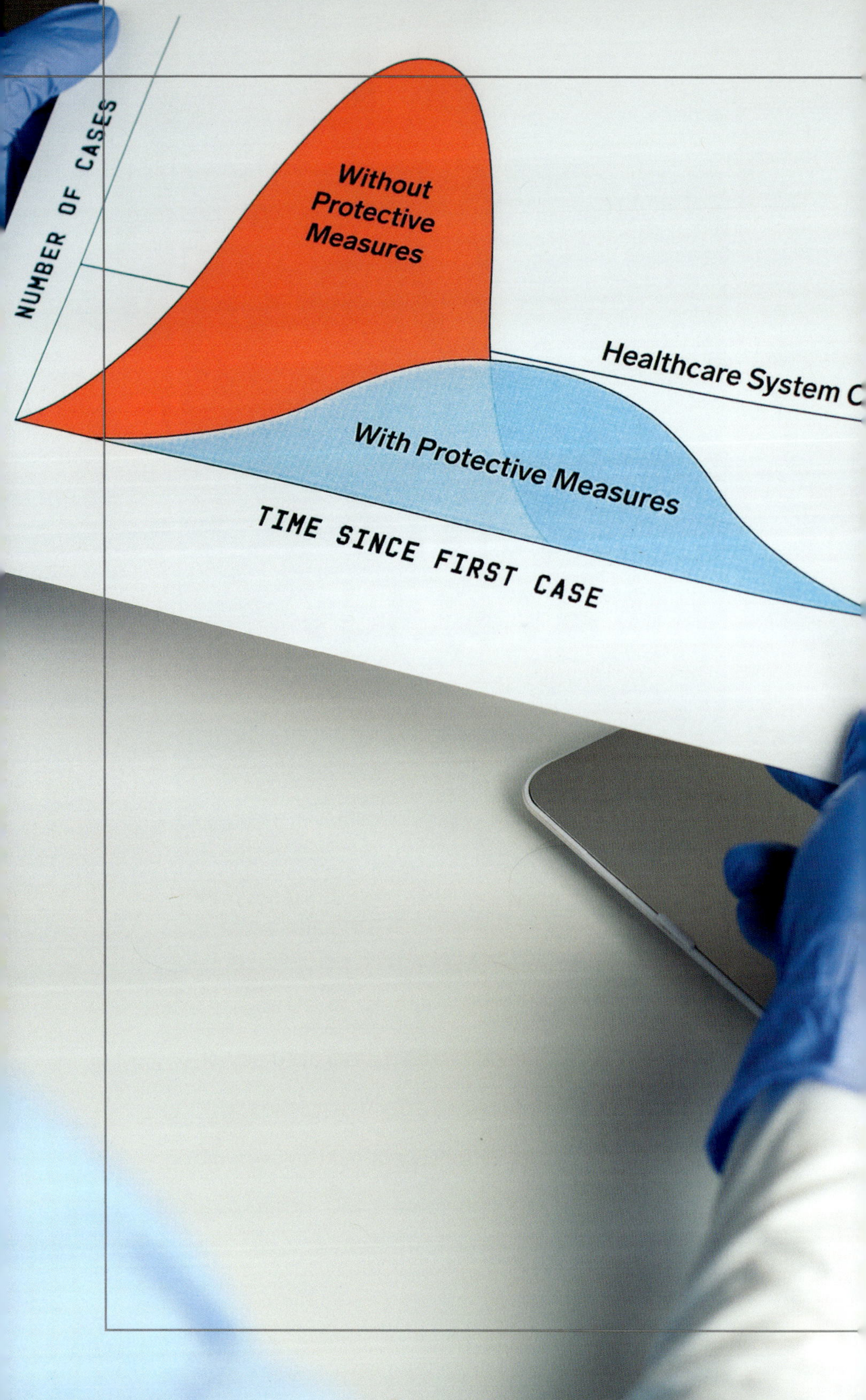

NUMBER OF CASES
Without Protective Measures
Healthcare System C
With Protective Measures
TIME SINCE FIRST CASE

FLATTEN THE CURVE

As cases began to rise across the United States in early 2020, sick patients flooded hospitals, taking a toll on the health-care system. Governments enacted rules to help flatten the curve. Flattening the curve meant slowing the spread of the virus and reducing the number of infections at one time to decrease the strain on the health-care system. Communities across the United States went to great lengths to answer the call.

As COVID-19 spread, authorities called for social distancing. Social distancing included staying away from people outside of one's household whenever possible and keeping at least six feet (1.8 m) away from others when outside of the home. As businesses and restaurants began reopening to limited in-person services, it was recommended that people continue with social distancing any time they were outside of the home and around other people in the community.

Flattening the curve meant spreading out the number of COVID-19 cases over a longer period of time so there were fewer cases at any given time.

In some places, reopened restaurants only allowed outdoor dining. Some set up structures that further protected diners from people at neighboring tables.

Reopenings varied from state to state. Some began reopening as early as the end of May 2020, but others waited to ease restrictions until July 2020.

Anyone with COVID-19 symptoms or who had been around someone who tested positive for COVID-19 was asked to self-quarantine. This involved staying home and away from others for 14 days. The CDC also recommended that anyone who traveled should self-quarantine for 14 days in case of infection or exposure.[1] Hawaii and other states temporarily made self-quarantine mandatory for travelers.

Many hospitals, outpatient medical facilities, and nursing homes limited or banned visitors to reduce exposure. Some even closed waiting rooms and common areas. On the positive side, this may have reduced community transmission of COVID-19, but there were many downsides to the new policies. Visits with loved ones are essential to overall health, and hospitalized patients and nursing home residents suffered from isolation both mentally and physically. Many people died alone during the pandemic, and loved ones didn't have the chance to say goodbye in person.

SUFFERING ALONE

As hospitals and nursing homes locked visitors out and kept patients and residents in, the standard of care came into question. Family members could no longer advocate for their loved ones. Some elderly patients were left in bed for days at a time. Others showed a significant decline in their conditions including weight loss, dehydration, and general emotional distress. It wasn't just the patients who suffered without visitors. The presence of loved ones helped medical staff as well by performing basic tasks such as hygiene, feeding, helping patients change clothes, and general supervision.

Masks also played a key role in preventing illness. Initially, the CDC and other health organizations did not recommend masks, but they changed their stance as the number of cases increased. Even before the recommendations changed, Americans were masking up. Shortages of masks were already a problem in March 2020, creating supply issues. Hospitals and health-care facilities across the country struggled to find enough PPE. To ease the strain, officials suggested the general public wear cloth face coverings to prevent the spread of infection. People began using bandanas, gaiters, and homemade cloth masks.

SORRY, WE'RE CLOSED

Offices and schools closed down in March 2020, asking everyone to stay at home. The initial plan proposed by President Trump called for a two-week shutdown of everything other than essential businesses.[2]

Essential businesses included grocery stores, home and

auto repair companies, gas stations, pharmacies, medical

centers, post offices, and food production facilities.

The effort to flatten
the curve meant limiting
contact with others.
Many people used
delivery or curbside
pickup options to get
groceries and other
products from stores.
By the middle of 2021,
people could find
designated parking spots
at many major stores and
restaurants for them to
call in for their orders to
be delivered to their cars
contact-free.

EXPLAINING MASKS

The WHO and the CDC changed their original stance on wearing masks. Doctors and scientists across the country had differing opinions as well. The CDC's website originally stated that only caretakers and people who were sick should consider wearing masks, but that advice later changed. Universal masking became highly recommended when scientists discovered that people without symptoms could spread COVID-19. If people covered their mouths and noses, even with a cloth mask, they would reduce the amount of infected particles released into the air.

With dining rooms closed, restaurants were forced

to transition to carryout, drive-through, and delivery

only. Orders were called in or placed online, and pickup

or delivery was a quick exchange. Delivery apps such as

SHOPPING ONLINE

During COVID-19, sales at some retailers rose significantly. Walmart reported a 10 percent increase in sales, with online purchases growing by more than 70 percent. Target reported that curbside pickup, in-store pickup, and delivery grew 278 percent.[4] Amazon reported record highs between April and June 2020, with online sales jumping 40 percent.[5] Even grocery shopping went digital, with 79 percent of consumers ordering groceries online by late May 2020.[6] However, the rise in online shopping mainly benefited large companies. It hurt many small businesses that did not already have online sales options. There were many struggles with adding online sales, including the need for additional space to manage the packaging and shipping of online orders—space many small businesses didn't have.

DoorDash, Postmates, and Uber Eats were used to get meals, and many people turned to shopping online to get what they needed, from toilet paper and disinfecting wipes to clothes and furniture.

When stay-at-home orders were extended into April and May 2020, schools and businesses were asked to transition to a virtual format, with employees and students working from their home computers. After a few false starts in trying to put students back in the classroom long-term, most schools had returned to in-person instruction by the fall of 2021, with many offering virtual instruction as an alternative. Many employees returned to the office, but for some, the office looked different. Mask requirements, partitions, and limited numbers of people on-site were just some of the changes. Some businesses required regular testing to ensure that infected employees didn't go into work. That way, they wouldn't spread the virus to others.

COVID-19 VARIANTS

Like most viruses, the original COVID-19 strain produced new variants. Detected in Great Britain in November 2020, Alpha was the first variant. Alpha made its way to the United States but was soon overtaken by the Delta variant, which was first identified in December 2020 in India and was thought to be twice as contagious. The new strain impacted younger people more frequently than the original strain. The Omicron variant appeared in November 2021 and was first identified in South Africa. It began spreading rapidly, indicating that it was also more contagious than previous variants, although the severity was yet to be determined. By mid-December 2021, Omicron was the dominant strain. And at the beginning of January 2022, researchers discovered a new variant in France. They kept a close eye on it to see if it would be more transmissible or cause a worse case of COVID-19 than past variants.

CHAPTER SIX

FIGHTING FROM THE FRONT LINES

Essential and frontline workers were at the core of the fight against COVID-19. While many people stayed home during the pandemic, basic needs still had to be met. Grocery stores were still staffed with employees so shoppers could get what they needed. Restaurants still maintained limited staff to serve delivery and takeout to customers. Gas stations still needed to operate. Law enforcement and firefighters continued to serve the needs of the community. But people in health-care professions handled COVID-19 most directly every day.

Medical professionals suited up in PPE to care for the sick and injured. Hospitals across the country saw an influx of patients, and many states developed temporary overflow facilities to accommodate them. The New York City Convention Center temporarily

Food warehouse workers were among the frontline workers who had to continue going into work during lockdowns.

housed 1,000 hospital beds.[1] California opened temporary field hospitals across the state at locations such as sports arenas and college campuses to care for patients who did not need to be in intensive care units.

Patients with mild symptoms were sent home, but the severely ill required beds and other medical equipment. During the pandemic, hospitals struggled with shortages of many medical supplies, including N95 face masks and sanitizer. Ventilators became another issue. Many patients suffered impaired lung function from COVID-19 infections, and ventilators were a way to provide a normal flow of air and oxygen for those struggling to breathe. Oxygen is needed for all bodily functions. As more patients suffered respiratory distress, hospitals faced a shortage of these important machines.

In late March 2020, President Trump asked vehicle manufacturing companies to produce essential PPE and ventilators without him needing to use the Defense Production Act. This act allows the federal government to require companies to prioritize making supplies for the government in the case of a national emergency. Ford, General Motors, General Electric, Hill-Rom, Medtronic, ResMed, Royal Philips, Vyaire Medical, and 3M all pitched in. Their efforts produced millions of face masks and nearly 100,000 ventilators.[3]

For people with mild symptoms who were able to recover at home, treatment was the same as for a cold or the flu. Officials recommended taking

The Defense Production Act was first established in 1950 during the Korean War (1950–1953). It helped the US military get supplies for the war by making companies prioritize government purchases over purchases from private companies or individuals. Since its creation, the US government has used this act many times when purchasing things such as tanks and bomber planes for the military. FEMA has also used it to quickly get supplies such as food and water to disaster sites.

over-the-counter pain relievers, drinking plenty of fluids, and getting enough rest. For those who were hospitalized, treatment was somewhat experimental in the early days of the pandemic. In 2020, the FDA allowed emergency use of the antiviral drug remdesivir and the drug baricitinib, a drug that has anti-inflammatory properties and is typically used for rheumatoid arthritis. There were several other treatment options under investigation, including additional antiviral drugs, corticosteroids, anti-inflammatory therapy, and immune-based therapy.

To reduce the possibility of transmission, hospitals banned visitors, closed emergency rooms and waiting areas, and donned extensive amounts of PPE such as gowns and masks. Because of supply shortages, some doctors and nurses wore the same N95 masks for multiple days, and at one point, professionals in New York wore trash bags as gowns. PPE is important to protect health-care workers from contracting the infection and to prevent contamination from one patient to another. When a mask is worn over and over again, it becomes less effective, putting both the health-care worker and the patients at higher risk.

Some companies shifted some of their resources to making PPE such as hospital gowns to help address the shortage.

HOSPITAL CONDITIONS

At the beginning of the pandemic, hospital admissions dropped in some places. Many hospitals chose to put elective surgeries and noncritical medical services on hold to accommodate the potential influx of patients infected with COVID-19 and to prevent the potential for spreading the virus. As COVID-19 surged, patients with severe infections began filling hospitals. Medical facilities reported many challenges. In addition to the shortage of PPE, there were also shortages of testing supplies, long wait times for test results, not enough spaces to treat patients, and even staff shortages. After working long, stressful days, some health-care workers quit after struggling with burnout.

—Unnamed nurse from a hospital on Long Island, New York, in March 2020

To help ease the burden, two US Navy hospital ships were deployed to New York City and Los Angeles to support the health-care crisis. Each ship provided approximately 1,000 beds, and their mission was to serve urgent care patients who were not infected with COVID-19.[4] The USNS *Mercy* arrived in Los Angeles on March 27, 2020, and the USNS *Comfort* docked in New York Harbor on March 30. *Comfort* left New York a month after arrival, having treated 182 patients, and *Mercy* left Los Angeles on May 15 after treating only 77 noninfected patients.[5] These numbers were low because *Comfort* and *Mercy* were intended to treat patients with

The USNS *Mercy* came to the Port of Los Angeles to treat urgent care patients who did not have a COVID-19 infection.

conditions other than COVID-19. With people staying home, there were fewer patients with workplace injuries or injuries such as those from car accidents.

The navy ships were not the only way the military supported the fight on the front lines during the pandemic. In November 2020 and continuing through 2021, military doctors were deployed directly to hospitals to assist with staff shortages. National Guard members built shelters for patients, distributed medical supplies, and provided assistance with testing and vaccinations. The Army Corps of Engineers converted buildings into temporary medical facilities.

OTHER FRONTLINE WORKERS

Health-care workers weren't the only frontline workers. People in a wide variety of occupations faced an increased risk of becoming ill with COVID-19 every time they showed up for work. These people included grocers, butchers, custodians, sanitation workers, and truck drivers. These people could not work from home, and their jobs were necessary to keep people fed and healthy. Because these workers often received low wages and had a high risk of exposure, they were among the most likely to get seriously ill or die from COVID-19 due to a lack of access to health care.

Frontline workers faced a greater risk of getting COVID-19 than workers who could do their jobs at home.

Early in 2020, some large businesses offered temporary pay increases or bonuses to frontline workers. Amazon gave workers a temporary raise of an additional two dollars per hour.[9] Walmart gave cash bonuses. But over the summer, many companies ended those benefits as media attention shifted away, the higher federal unemployment payments ended, and more people were looking for jobs. In March 2021, President Biden signed the American Rescue Plan into law. It included money that state and local governments could give to frontline workers as hazard pay. However, the funding was not enough for all frontline workers, and governments struggled to decide who would receive the payments.

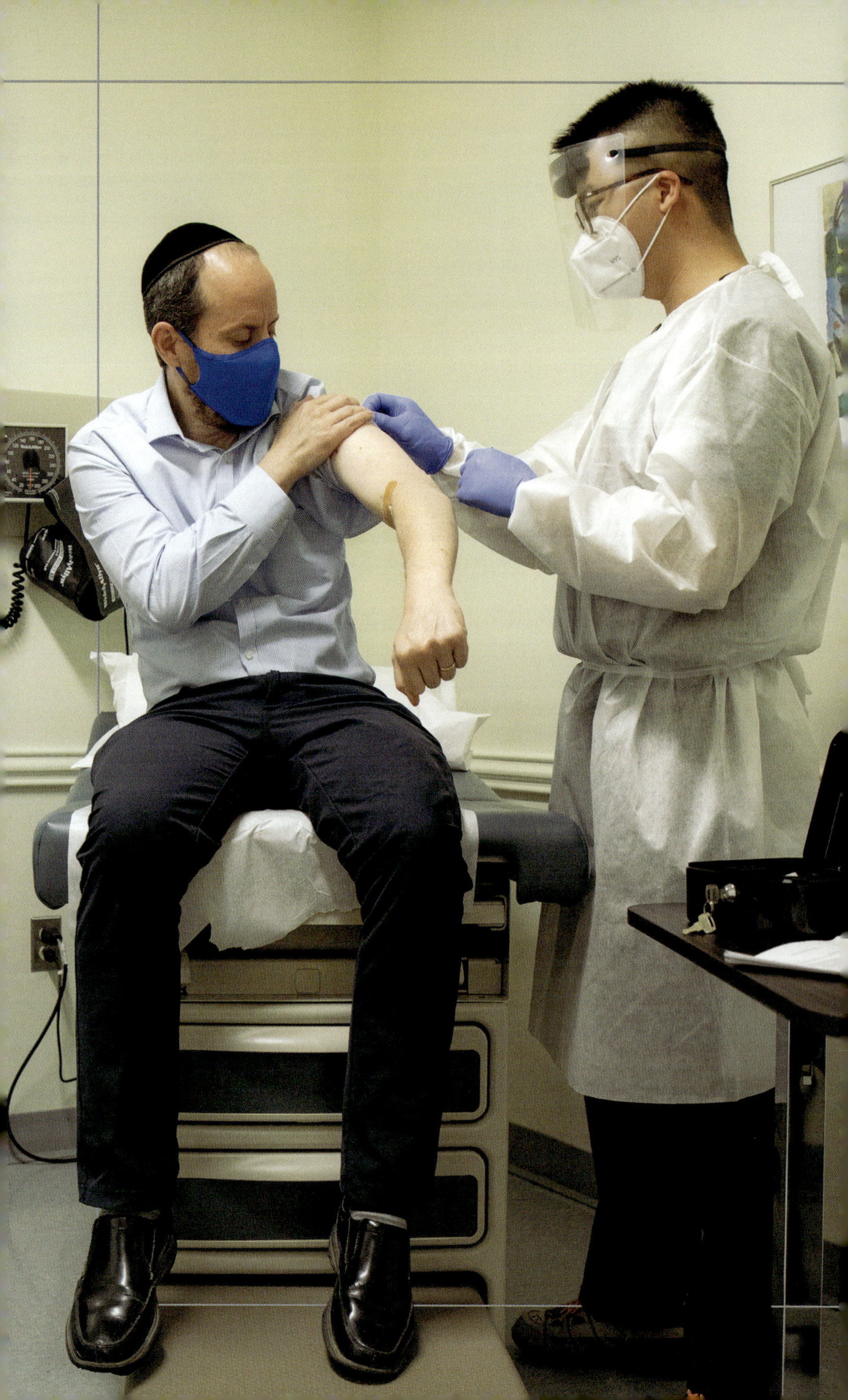

CHAPTER SEVEN

THE VACCINES

For the first time in history, a vaccine against a new disease was created, tested, and authorized for use in less than one year. Fortunately, the virus that causes COVID-19 is part of a family of coronaviruses that scientists had been researching for years. This gave researchers a head start.

The process of vaccine development involved several steps. First, scientists needed to make it. Then the vaccine needed to go through three phases of clinical trials. After clinical trials, the vaccine needed authorization or approval by government agencies. Once approved, manufacturing and distribution were required to get the vaccine to market. All of this took time and money. The Trump administration took action to accelerate the development process while ensuring that none of the important safety steps were skipped.

Many Americans volunteered for COVID-19 vaccine clinical trials, which tested the safety and effectiveness of the vaccines in humans before the vaccines were widely distributed.

President Trump announced OWS on May 15, 2020. This was a federal effort to accelerate the development and distribution of supplies and treatment, including a vaccine, for COVID-19. By May 21, there was a $1.2 billion contract with drug company AstraZeneca. With a contract, the government would give AstraZeneca the specified sum of money to help fund research and development of a vaccine, and in return it would receive 300 million doses of its vaccine when it had been approved.[1] Additional contracts followed with Novavax, Johnson & Johnson, Sanofi-GSK, Merck, Moderna, and Pfizer-BioNTech. By July, Moderna and Pfizer were already testing their COVID-19 vaccines on people who volunteered to participate in clinical trials, and Johnson & Johnson followed in September.

The goal of OWS was to get 20 million people vaccinated by the end of 2020, or at least get the first of the two required doses. But it wasn't until December 11 that the FDA gave EUA to the first vaccine, which was made by Pfizer. Moderna's vaccine received authorization on December 18, 2020. The first dose of a vaccine given in the United States was administered on December 14, 2020, to nurse Sandra Lindsay at Long Island Jewish

Medical Center in New York.

By December 31, just under three million people had received a shot. The federal government distributed the vaccines to the states, but the pace of vaccination was slow. This was due in part to the lack of funds to hire staff to administer the vaccines. In addition, vaccination sites had to limit the number of people receiving a vaccine at the same time to maintain social distancing and prevent the spread of disease. And it took time to manufacture enough vaccines for everyone.

Because of these limitations, governments gave priority to certain people at first, such as health-care

DEVELOPING THE VACCINES

Some people were concerned with how quickly the COVID-19 vaccines were developed. They worried that corners had been cut, risking the safety of the vaccines. A Connecticut Department of Health pamphlet explained why this was not the case. It said that research into vaccines effective against coronaviruses had already been underway for many years after SARS and MERS epidemics in 2003 and 2012 killed a number of people. In addition, researchers followed the standard FDA process, including research, animal trials, three phases of human clinical trials, and application for FDA approval. Funding played a big role in developing the vaccines quickly. Vaccine development is an expensive process. But because COVID-19 was so deadly globally, researchers received enough funding to prioritize the research.

workers and residents of long-term care facilities. This ensured that the vaccines would be administered to those who were most at risk for exposure and severe complications from coronavirus infection. As a result, many people who wanted a vaccine were unable to get one in the first months because they didn't meet eligibility requirements.

The first-priority groups included frontline health-care workers and nursing home residents. The second group included people who worked in essential roles such as law enforcement, fire services, education, transportation, and food and agriculture. The third group included people with health conditions that put them at high risk for serious complications related to COVID-19. The fourth group included adults 65 and older. It wasn't until the end of April 2021 that the vaccines were available for all people older than age 18.

mRNA VACCINES

There were three vaccines available to Americans in 2021. The Pfizer and Moderna vaccines had both been authorized for emergency use in December 2020. The third vaccine, made by Johnson & Johnson, received

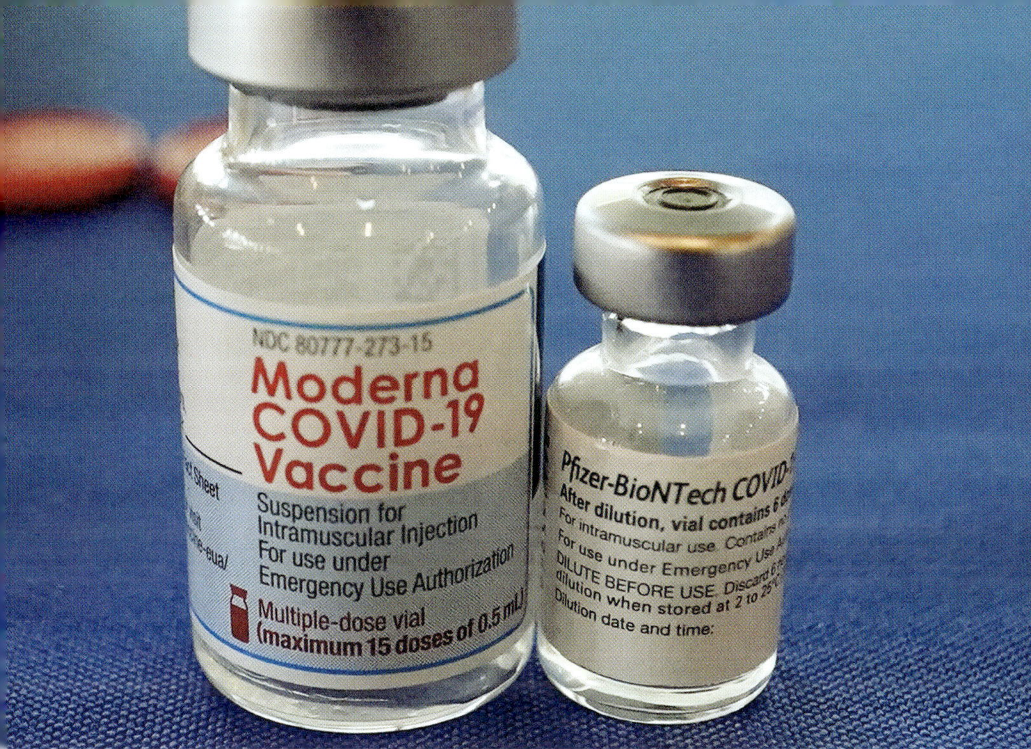

The Pfizer and Moderna vaccines were the first mRNA vaccines made and authorized for use in the United States.

authorization on February 27, 2021. The initial vaccine rollout was available only for adults, but by the end of the year there were vaccines under EUA that were available for everyone five and older. The Pfizer vaccine received full FDA approval in August 2021 for adults, even outside of emergency use.

The Pfizer vaccine required two shots 21 days apart. The Moderna vaccine required two shots 28 days apart.[2] People with weakened immune systems were urged to get a third dose. The Pfizer vaccine was authorized for children five and up on October 29, 2021.[3]

VACCINE ADVERSE EVENT REPORTING SYSTEM

The Vaccine Adverse Event Reporting System (VAERS) was established in 1990 under HHS. VAERS tracks adverse reactions to vaccines to identify safety issues. Health-care workers and vaccine developers are required to report to VAERS any adverse effects observed after vaccination. However, anyone can file a report through VAERS, and an adverse event does not need to be clearly connected with a vaccine to report it. For this reason, the system cannot be used to determine with certainty that a vaccine is dangerous. Instead, it is useful for detecting patterns of adverse effects to be further researched for safety concerns.

The Pfizer and Moderna vaccines are messenger ribonucleic acid (mRNA) vaccines. These vaccines contain the mRNA genetic code for a spike protein on the COVID-19 virus. When injected, the mRNA code enters the body's cells and tells them to make the harmless spike protein. The body's immune system recognizes the spike protein as a foreign substance in the body, prompting an immune response. The immune system will remember the spike protein and how to neutralize it if the body is later infected with SARS-CoV-2. It will be able to respond more quickly to the virus than if it hadn't received a vaccine, reducing the likelihood of infection or severe disease. Common side effects for both mRNA vaccines included fever, chills, headaches, and fatigue, and they were usually more severe after the second dose.

The FDA added warning labels to the Pfizer vaccine after cases of myocarditis and pericarditis, inflammation of the heart or the outer lining of the heart, were reported by young adults and adolescents after taking the vaccine. There were also reports of myocarditis and pericarditis with the Moderna vaccine, so this one received an FDA warning label as well. These side effects were rare, seen in about 12.6 cases for every one million second doses administered.[4] And most times, the side effects go away on their own.

JOHNSON & JOHNSON

On February 27, 2021, the FDA authorized the Janssen vaccine by Johnson & Johnson for emergency use for everyone 18 and older. Unlike the mRNA vaccines, it required just one shot.[5] The Janssen vaccine works similarly to other traditional vaccines on the market and contains a modified, harmless virus that carries genetic instructions for the SARS-CoV-2 spike protein. Cells in the body produce the spike protein, triggering an immune response in the body, which creates antibodies that provide protection from later infections.

Common side effects included fever, headaches, muscle aches, and fatigue. This vaccine was reinvestigated after reports of a blood clotting disorder occurred in some patients, and other patients developed Guillain-Barré syndrome, a neurological disorder. An FDA warning label was added for these two issues.

BREAKTHROUGH INFECTIONS AND BOOSTER SHOTS

When the vaccines came out, many people hoped that if everyone got vaccinated, the virus would be eliminated. The campaign to vaccinate all eligible adults rolled out. Across social media, people used stickers and profile picture frames to announce when they were vaccinated, urging their friends to stop the spread and get vaccinated too.

But mutations of the original virus emerged, and the vaccines were not as effective against these variants. Vaccinated people continued to get infected with COVID-19, and some were even hospitalized. Some people who were fully vaccinated died from the disease.

Some people posted pictures online of themselves with stickers that said they had been vaccinated against COVID-19.

However, the vaccines still greatly reduced the risk of hospitalization or death from COVID-19. For example, Minnesota recorded 16.8 deaths in unvaccinated people per 100,000 people during the week of December 26, 2021, but just 1.2 deaths in fully vaccinated people per 100,000.[6]

Due to the decline of antibodies over time and the appearance of new variants, booster shots were recommended in fall 2021 for all vaccinated people.

People could mix and match the shots. So they may have had the Pfizer series initially, but they could get any one of the three vaccines as the booster. The boosters were intended to create more antibodies to protect against infection from SARS-CoV-2 and the mutations that had emerged. The CDC suggested a booster shot for Pfizer-BioNTech and Moderna at least five months after the first set of shots and a booster at least two months after the initial dose for the Johnson & Johnson vaccine.[7] At-risk people would be eligible for an additional booster following a similar time frame recommendation for the first booster.[8]

At the end of March 2022, 11.26 percent of the US population was partially vaccinated, and more than 65 percent was fully vaccinated. For every 100 people, 28 booster shots had been given. At the same time, more than 23 percent of the US population remained unvaccinated.[9] There were many reasons people chose not to get vaccinated. Some people don't think any vaccine is safe. Others were concerned with the speed at which the COVID-19 vaccines had been developed and wanted to wait and see how the vaccines affected other people before being vaccinated themselves.

Data showed the vaccines were very safe. Just three confirmed cases of thrombosis with thrombocytopenia syndrome (TTS), a serious blood clotting event, had occurred after receiving the Moderna vaccine by March 2022. At that time, more than 540 million doses of mRNA vaccines had been given. The Johnson & Johnson vaccine carried a higher risk of TTS. Sixty people developed TTS after getting this vaccine. At the time, 18.5 million doses had been given. Overall, by March 2022, 0.0024 percent of people who had received a vaccine had died afterward.[10] However, not all of these deaths were necessarily from the vaccines. Health-care workers are required to report any death after vaccination, even when it's unclear that vaccination was the cause. By comparison, in the United States, 1.2 percent of people infected with COVID-19 died.[11]

Heated comments between the vaccinated and unvaccinated were common on Facebook and Twitter. People unfriended or unfollowed each other because of their stance on vaccines. While the divide continued, so did the pandemic.

MANDATORY VACCINE POLICY

President Biden pushed for new vaccine requirements in an effort to end the pandemic more quickly. In July 2021, Biden rolled out a vaccine requirement for federal employees and contractors. Then, in November 2021, he mandated that all federal employees and all businesses with more than 100 employees require full vaccination or regular testing.[13] Unvaccinated employees would be required to wear masks. The Occupational Safety and Health Administration (OSHA) would oversee the business mandate. Health-care workers at facilities that took payments from Medicare and Medicaid were also required to get fully vaccinated. The businesses and health-care workers were to be vaccinated by January 4, 2022. The military likewise required full vaccination, or service members could face release from the military and the loss of important government benefits.

Many people were vaccinated following these mandates. Others disagreed with the requirements, and some of these people filed lawsuits against vaccine policies. Ten states filed a lawsuit against the Biden administration over vaccine mandates for health-care workers.[14] They argued that terminating employment of unvaccinated health-care workers would increase the shortage of medical personnel. In January 2020, the US Supreme Court ruled that Biden could not mandate vaccines for businesses with more than 100 employees. However, the federal government could require vaccines at medical facilities that take Medicare and Medicaid payments.

"Although Congress has indisputably given OSHA the power to regulate occupational dangers, it has not given that agency the power to regulate public health more broadly. Requiring the vaccination of 84 million Americans, selected simply because they work for employers with more than 100 employees, certainly falls in the latter category."[15]

—*The US Supreme Court's statement about overturning President Biden's vaccine mandate for businesses*

Due to
tight supply,
limit 2 per
customer.
Paper Goods/ Cleaning
Supplies/ Bulk Water
STOP&SHOP

$2.29
EVERYDAY
LOW
PRICE

THE PEOPLE FIGHT THE PANDEMIC

When COVID-19 reached pandemic levels, there was an initial sense of panic. Fear of catching the virus or of being stuck at home for an extended time led to crowded stores where people hoarded toilet paper, canned goods, and disinfectants. But as the situation evolved, so did people's responses to it.

As consumers calmed down with stockpiling, it took time for manufacturers and the supply chain to catch up. Toilet paper was one of the primary things that was difficult to find for the first several weeks. People asked around online about which stores had toilet paper in stock. Others stepped up to share some of their own supply. Some neighbors even set up their own front yard pantries with canned goods, toilet paper, donated

Shelves that were once filled with products such as toilet paper quickly emptied in early 2020 as COVID-19 hit the United States.

A BREATH OF FRESH AIR

At the beginning of the pandemic, playgrounds were roped off, beaches were closed to the public, and golf courses were shut down. Officials didn't want people gathering, even in outdoor spaces. When the stay-at-home orders loosened, many outdoor areas opened for the public to enjoy once again. Transmission rates were low outdoors, and though social distancing and masks were still required, people were free to begin using hiking trails and beaches. People started getting outside more frequently, and outdoor recreation items became hot sellers. Bicycles, skateboards, and roller skates were often sold out.

clothing, and other items that people in the community may have needed.

There were often people lined up at the door before grocery stores even opened, waiting for their chance to grab the restocked supply of goods before the store was once again cleared out. Many stores implemented senior hours for people older than 65.[1] These early morning hours were times when only seniors were allowed into the store to shop without having to battle the crowds. This gave them a chance to get the supplies they needed in a safer environment with less exposure to potentially infected people.

Facing a shortage of masks, many people across the country began making homemade face coverings. They became top-selling products on Etsy, an online marketplace where people can sell things they make.

Some made masks to give to friends and family for free, while others sold them from tables in their front yards. Some people also made 3D printed face shields.

SLOWING THE SPREAD

Many people took measures to stay safe and slow the spread of the virus. Birthdays and holidays are normally times for gathering. During the pandemic, people were isolating and keeping a distance from their community, friends, and even family members who lived in separate households. Celebrations transitioned to drive-by parties. People decorated their cars with birthday banners, honked their horns, and waved as they slowly drove by the home of the person being celebrated. This limited interaction was an opportunity for people to see loved

WHERE'S THE TOILET PAPER?

The demand for toilet paper being purchased for homes increased by 112 percent in March 2020 compared with March 2019.[2] Before COVID-19, people were at work or school for a large part of the day. When the stay-at-home orders went into effect, people were using their own bathrooms more frequently, so more toilet paper was needed at home. But toilet paper manufacturers did not make enough toilet paper to meet the new demand. As the supply of toilet paper got lower, people started buying more than what they needed to be sure they didn't run out, causing a shortage. In response, stores limited purchases to one package per customer, and factories ramped up production to meet the demand.

ones and bring a smile to each other's faces. During 2020, it wasn't uncommon to see caravans of cars filtering past a child in a party hat in their front yard, horns honking and people shouting greetings as they drove by.

Virtual communication became commonplace during the pandemic as people quarantined in their homes and switched to telecommuting for work and remote learning for school. Zoom became a household name. The videoconferencing platform allowed teachers to connect with their students, businesses to conduct office meetings, and families to chat from their living rooms. Video calls from smartphones and tablets became a popular way for people to keep in touch with friends and family.

Businesses, especially restaurants, got creative with ways to provide for their communities. Many restaurants and businesses receive regular preordered shipments of

People decorated their vehicles for drive-by parties as a creative way to celebrate while maintaining social distancing.

food and paper goods. With fewer customers and staff, they often had a surplus of products. Restaurants started selling boxes with fresh fruit and vegetables, meat, bread, and even rolls of toilet paper. This helped provide income for the restaurant and allowed consumers to get necessary items without going to crowded stores.

COMMUNITY ENGAGEMENT

Museums, cultural centers, and other educational facilities found online ways to provide activities for people to engage with at home. The National Park Service, which normally welcomes millions of visitors per year to destinations all over the country, now saw empty parks. It pivoted and brought the outdoors to the people with virtual field trips, webcams, and multimedia galleries. It also offered games, virtual junior ranger programs for kids to earn badges, and activity ideas to keep kids busy and learning.

THE NEW NORMAL

During the pandemic, the closing of businesses across the country had a major impact on employment. In February 2020, before the pandemic struck the United States, unemployment rates were at 3.8 percent, one of the lowest rates on record since World War II (1939–1945).[1] In April 2020, the unemployment rate climbed to 14.7 percent.[2]

To ease the financial strain, the Trump administration rolled out the CARES Act with its stimulus payments. But the stimulus checks didn't solve the unemployment problem. People were still out of work. As businesses reopened and vaccination rates climbed, more people rejoined the workforce. However, at the end of 2021, many businesses were struggling with staff shortages. And even with a higher rate of unemployment, more Americans were quitting their jobs, starting their own businesses, or retiring. In April 2021 alone, four million

The Ohio National Guard helped food banks in the state during the pandemic. Rising unemployment rates meant more people needed food banks.

people walked away from their jobs.[3] In July 2021, there were more available jobs than there were workers who wanted to fill them. Several factors played into the staff shortages. Many open jobs were low-paying, some workers no longer wanted to commute, and some people were choosing to continue with social distancing to prevent becoming infected with COVID-19. While the economy continued to slowly grow, the job market was unpredictable, and the full effect of unemployment during the pandemic was yet to be determined.

SCHOOLS AND BUSINESSES

The pandemic continued, and the virus mutated, but Americans wanted to get back to normal, or at least to a new normal. What that looked like varied from state to state, and sometimes even from one community to the next. Schools and businesses opened back up after lockdowns, but new safety measures were implemented. Masks were mandatory, and many places required vaccinations. Some safety measures seen in schools and businesses included plexiglass partitions, social distancing, frequent cleaning, and better ventilation systems. Some businesses and schools continued to offer remote options.

Restaurants and retail stores opened back up for regular dining and shopping, many requiring masks for the unvaccinated. Masks could be removed while eating. Mask policies were not always strictly enforced

COVID FATIGUE

COVID fatigue is a general sense of feeling exhausted or emotionally drained from dealing with the issues and challenges associated with the ongoing COVID-19 pandemic. As people faced long-term isolation, joblessness, and overwhelming amounts of information about the disease, exhaustion and stress set in. People were losing their optimism. Americans began to experience depression, anxiety, and lack of motivation. Health-care workers were especially worn out from the strain of dealing firsthand with sick and dying patients. Many began to experience insomnia, depression, anxiety, and burnout. To cope with COVID fatigue, experts recommended exercising, talking with others about the frustrations of pandemic life, practicing mindfulness through breathing or meditation, journaling, and limiting exposure to the news.

—*Kaye Hermanson, psychologist, UC Davis Health*

by the end of 2021, but signs were posted, and businesses varied on the degree to which they required masks for their customers and employees.

Events began filling calendars again, many shifting to outdoor venues to accommodate large crowds while reducing the potential for virus transmission. Events at indoor venues sometimes required proof of vaccination or proof of a negative COVID test to gain entry. Los Angeles had one of the stricter mandates. Everyone age 12 and older was required to show proof of vaccination to enter restaurants, bars, gyms, entertainment venues, barber shops, and other indoor facilities.

By mid-2021, a growing number of people were less afraid of the virus, though many still took measures to prevent being infected or spreading the disease. A new variant of the virus, called Omicron, emerged in November 2021. Omicron proved to be more contagious but less severe than previous variants. Researchers hoped that this less severe variant would help reduce the severity of future SARS-CoV-2 variants. Some experts believed that COVID-19 would become an endemic disease, meaning it will always be present but it will be manageable, and that high rates of previous infections and vaccinations will help reduce the death rate and lead to more time between new variants forming.

Researchers continued to work on developing treatments and vaccines that were more effective at treating or eliminating the virus, but there was no way of knowing when the pandemic would end. People were tired of the challenges that came with pandemic life. It was clear that the virus wasn't going anywhere. So Americans continued to look for new ways of living with it.

ESSENTIAL FACTS

KEY EVENTS

- On January 22, 2020, the WHO confirms human-to-human spread of COVID-19.

- The first COVID-19 diagnostic tests are distributed in the United States on February 4, 2020.

- On March 1, 2020, the CDC begins tracking the number of COVID-19 tests performed daily.

- On March 16, 2020, a 15-day nationwide plan to slow the spread of coronavirus begins, with many schools and businesses across the country closing their doors.

- In April 2020, the first round of stimulus checks is distributed to qualifying Americans.

- The first COVID-19 vaccine administered for public use is given December 14, 2020.

- By March 2022, more than 65 percent of the US population is fully vaccinated.

KEY PEOPLE

- As president of the United States from the beginning of the pandemic through January 20, 2021, Donald Trump took actions to accelerate vaccine development and encourage businesses across the country to ramp up production of much-needed personal protective equipment.

- Beginning January 21, 2021, President Joe Biden took on the fight against the coronavirus by increasing vaccination efforts and continuing to ensure the availability of personal protective equipment and test kits.

- Dr. Anthony Fauci served as one of the leaders and health experts on the White House Coronavirus Task Force

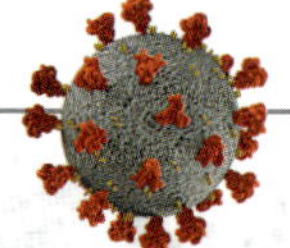

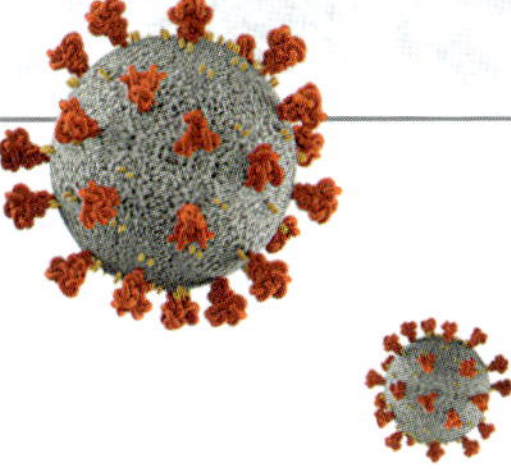

and was often the face of the updates regarding the COVID-19 pandemic. He helped provide guidance to the American public.

KEY STATISTICS

- Approximately 50 million US children shifted to remote learning during the COVID-19 pandemic.

- The demand for home toilet paper increased 112 percent in March 2020 compared with March 2019.

- By April 2020, more than 14 percent of the American workforce was unemployed because of business closures and other issues related to the pandemic.

- Grocery shopping went digital, with 79 percent of consumers shopping online for their groceries by late May 2020.

- There was a dramatic increase in people reporting symptoms of anxiety and depression during the pandemic, climbing to more than 40 percent in December 2020 from just 11 percent pre-pandemic.

- By the end of 2020, more than one million tests were being used daily, sometimes climbing to more than two million.

QUOTE

"This is not just a public health crisis, it is a crisis that will touch every sector—so every sector and every individual must be involved in the fight."

—Dr. Tedros Adhanom Ghebreyesus,
WHO director general, March 11, 2020

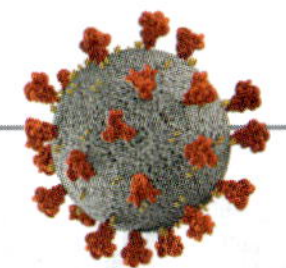

GLOSSARY

antibody
A protein that the immune system uses to fight infection.

community transmission
The spread of a disease or illness from person to person within a community.

contact tracing
A process used to identify people who have been in contact with someone who was diagnosed with an infectious illness for the purpose of treating or isolating them to prevent further spread.

emergency use authorization (EUA)
An authorization by the Food and Drug Administration that allows the use of a drug or treatment prior to full approval. EUA makes the product accessible during a state of emergency when no other viable alternative is available.

epidemic
The rapid spreading of a disease so that many people have it at the same time.

flatten the curve
To slow the spread of a disease and reduce the number of infected patients at a given time to ease the strain on the health-care system.

immune system
A bodily system that protects the body from foreign particles such as bacteria and viruses.

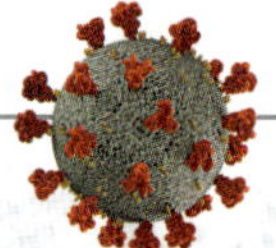

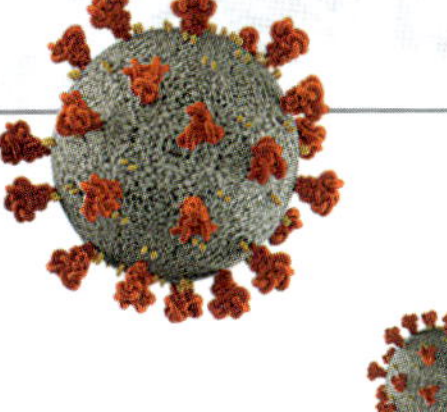

immunologist

A medical professional or doctor who diagnoses, treats, and works to prevent health issues caused by problems with the immune system.

personal protective equipment (PPE)

Supplies such as surgical masks, rubber gloves, and gowns that help prevent infection and are most often used by medical personnel.

quarantine

To physically isolate, particularly for people who are ill and possibly contagious.

social distancing

Keeping a safe distance from other people to avoid catching a disease.

vaccine

A drug that prevents or treats illness by stimulating the immune system to create antibodies.

variant

A strain of a virus that may contain one or more mutations.

whistleblower

Someone within a group or organization who reports issues that are illicit or inappropriate.

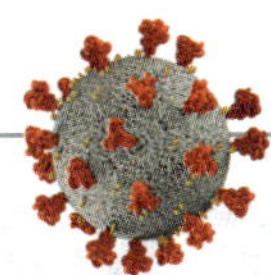

ADDITIONAL RESOURCES

SELECTED BIBLIOGRAPHY

"Anthony S. Fauci, M.D., NIAID Director." *National Institute of Allergy and Infectious Disease*, n.d., niaid.nih.gov. Accessed 13 Jan. 2022.

Katella, Kathy. "5 Things to Know about the Delta Variant." *Yale Medicine*, 6 Jan. 2022, yalemedicine.org. Accessed 13 Jan. 2022.

Shmerling, Robert H. "Which Test Is Best for COVID-19?" *Harvard Health Publishing*, 5 Jan. 2021, health.harvard.edu. Accessed 13 Jan. 2022.

FURTHER READINGS

Edwards, Sue Bradford. *Coronavirus: The COVID-19 Pandemic*. Abdo, 2021.

Hamen, Susan E. *Fighting COVID-19 Abroad*. Abdo, 2023.

Marrin, Albert. *Very, Very, Very Dreadful: The Influenza Pandemic of 1918*. Alfred A. Knopf, 2018.

ONLINE RESOURCES

To learn more about fighting COVID-19 in the United States, please visit **abdobooklinks.com** or scan this QR code. These links are routinely monitored and updated to provide the most current information available.

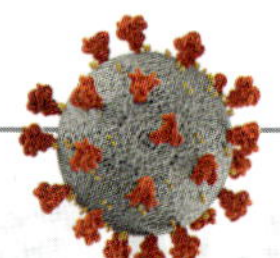

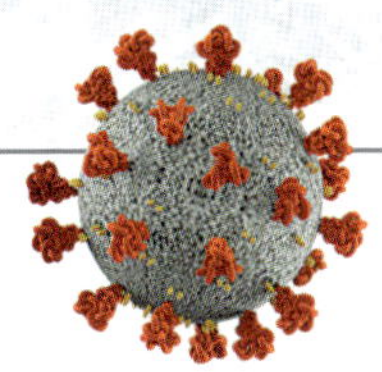

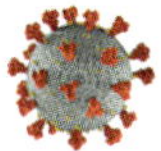

MORE INFORMATION

For more information on this subject, contact or visit the following organizations:

US CENTERS FOR DISEASE CONTROL AND PREVENTION (CDC)

1600 Clifton Rd.
Atlanta, GA 30329
1-800-232-4636
cdc.gov

The CDC played a key role in the COVID-19 response in the United States. It developed a test for the disease, and it provides scientific information on how to prevent the disease as well as what to do if infected.

US FOOD AND DRUG ADMINISTRATION (FDA)

10903 New Hampshire Ave.
Silver Spring, MD 20993
1-888-463-6332
fda.gov

The FDA evaluates food, drugs, and medical devices for safety and to ensure that the drugs and medical devices work. During the pandemic, the FDA evaluated and approved vaccines and drugs to prevent and treat COVID-19.

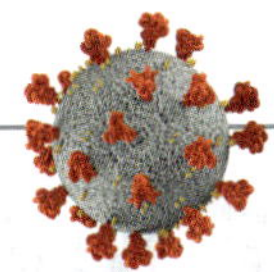

SOURCE NOTES

CHAPTER 1. PANDEMIC!

1. Dan Mangan. "Trump Issues 'Coronavirus Guidelines' for Next 15 Days to Slow Pandemic." *CNBC*, 16 Mar. 2020, cnbc.com. Accessed 30 Mar. 2022.

2. "Over 3,000 Cases in the U.S.; Airport Chaos Due to New Screenings." *NBC News*, 15 Mar. 2020, nbcnews.com. Accessed 30 Mar. 2022.

3. "Quotes of Fear, Defiance and Hope as the Coronavirus Pandemic Spans the Globe." *Reuters*, 28 June 2020, reuters.com. Accessed 30 Mar. 2022.

4. John Elflein. "Distribution of Total COVID-19 Deaths in the United States as of March 27, 2022, by Age Group." *Statista*, 28 Mar. 2022, statista.com. Accessed 30 Mar. 2022.

5. Smriti Mallapaty. "What the Cruise-Ship Outbreaks Reveal about COVID-19." *Nature*, 26 Mar. 2020, nature.com. Accessed 30 Mar. 2022.

6. Sharon Terlep. "Hand Sanitizer Sales Jumped 600% in 2020. Purell Maker Bets Against a Post-Pandemic Collapse." *Wall Street Journal*, 22 Jan. 2021, wsj.com. Accessed 30 Mar. 2022.

CHAPTER 2. OUTBREAKS PAST AND PRESENT

1. "1918 Pandemic (H1N1 Virus)." *CDC*, 20 Mar. 2019, cdc.gov. Accessed 30 Mar. 2022.

2. "2009 H1N1 Pandemic (H1N1pdm09 Virus)." *CDC*, 11 June 2019, cdc.gov. Accessed 30 Mar. 2022.

3. "Severe Acute Respiratory Syndrome (SARS)." *Johns Hopkins Medicine*, 2022, hopkinsmedicine.org. Accessed 30 Mar. 2022.

4. Yan Lianke. "Yan Lianke: What Happens After Coronavirus?" *Literary Hub*, 11 Mar. 2020, lithub.com. Accessed 30 Mar. 2022.

5. Jon Cohen. "Wuhan Seafood Market May Not Be Source of Novel Virus Spreading Globally." *Science*, 26 Jan. 2020, science.org. Accessed 30 Mar. 2022.

6. Jason Gale. "Delayed Wuhan Report Adds Crucial Detail to Covid Origin Puzzle." *Bloomberg*, 16 Aug. 2021, bloomberg.com. Accessed 30 Mar. 2022.

7. "Trends in Number of COVID-19 Cases and Deaths in the US Reported to CDC, by State/Territory." *CDC*, 28 Mar. 2022, covid.cdc.gov. Accessed 30 Mar. 2022.

8. "Totals for the US." *COVID Tracking Project*, 7 Mar. 2021, covidtracking.com. Accessed 30 Mar. 2022.

CHAPTER 3. WHO'S IN CHARGE?

1. "WHO Director-General's Opening Remarks at the Media Briefing on COVID-19." *WHO*, 11 Mar. 2020, who.int. Accessed 30 Mar. 2022.

2. "Children's Hospitals Toolkit." *We Can Do This*, 3 Nov. 2021, wecandothis.hhs.gov. Accessed 30 Mar. 2022.

3. Kelsey Snell. "What's Inside the Senate's $2 Trillion Coronavirus Aid Package." *NPR*, 26 Mar. 2020, npr.org. Accessed 30 Mar. 2022.

4. Eugene Kiely, Lori Robertson, Rem Rieder, and D'Angelo Gore. "Timeline of Trump's COVID-19 Comments." *FactCheck*, 2 Oct. 2020, factcheck.org. Accessed 30 Mar. 2022.

5. Selena Simmons-Duffin and Pien Huang. "A Year in, Experts Assess Biden's Hits and Misses on Handling the Pandemic." *NPR*, 18 Jan. 2022, npr.org. Accessed 30 Mar. 2022.

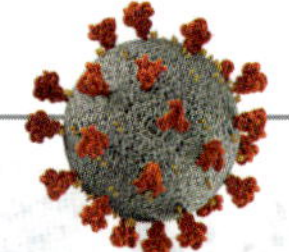

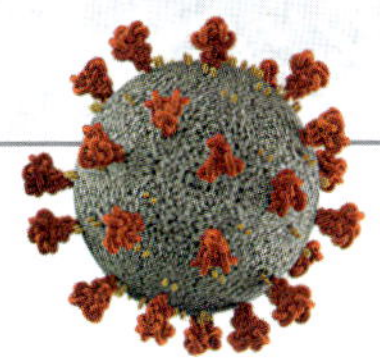
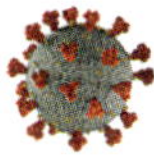

6. Salvador Rizzo. "Fauci Fires Back at Rand Paul, Accusing Him of Using Attacks for 'Political Gain.'" *Washington Post*, 11 Jan. 2022, washingtonpost.com. Accessed 30 Mar. 2022.

7. Alison Abbott. "COVID's Mental-Health Toll: How Scientists Are Tracking a Surge in Depression." *Nature*, 3 Feb. 2021, nature.com. Accessed 30 Mar. 2022.

8. Mark É. Czeisler et al. "Mental Health, Substance Use, and Suicidal Ideation During the COVID-19 Pandemic—United States, June 24–30, 2020." *CDC*, 14 Aug. 2020, cdc.gov. Accessed 30 Mar. 2022.

9. Brian Neelon et al. "As Cases Spread across U.S. Last Year, Pattern Emerged Suggesting Link between Governors' Party Affiliation and COVID-19 Case and Death Numbers." *Johns Hopkins*, 10 Mar. 2021, publichealth.jhu.edu. Accessed 30 Mar. 2022.

CHAPTER 4. TESTING, TESTING

1. "CDC Museum COVID-19 Timeline." *CDC*, 5 Jan. 2022, cdc.gov. Accessed 30 Mar. 2022.

2. Amanda Barrell. "How Long Does It Take to Get COVID-19 Test Results?" *Medical News Today*, 8 Sept. 2020, medicalnewstoday.com. Accessed 30 Mar. 2022.

3. Alden Gonzalez. "Dodger Stadium Now Largest Coronavirus Testing Site in California." *ESPN*, 26 May 2020, espn.com. Accessed 30 Mar. 2022.

4. Hannah Flynn. "Coronavirus Reinfection: How Long Might 'Natural Immunity' Last?" *Medical News Today*, 18 Oct. 2021, medicalnewstoday.com. Accessed 30 Mar. 2022.

5. "Trends in Number of COVID-19 Cases and Deaths in the US Reported to CDC, by State/Territory." *CDC*, 28 Mar. 2022, covid.cdc.gov. Accessed 30 Mar. 2022.

6. "Trends in Number of COVID-19 Cases and Deaths."

7. "Trends in Number of COVID-19 Cases and Deaths."

8. Dina Temple-Raston. "CDC Report: Officials Knew Coronavirus Test Was Flawed But Released It Anyway." *NPR*, 6 Nov. 2020, npr.org. Accessed 30 Mar. 2022.

9. Neel V. Patel. "Why the CDC Botched Its Coronavirus Testing." *Technology Review*, 5 Mar. 2020, technologyreview.com. Accessed 30 Mar. 2022.

10. "Totals for the US." *COVID Tracking Project*, 7 Mar. 2021, covidtracking.com. Accessed 30 Mar. 2022.

11. Emily Hoeven. "State Renews $1.7 Billion Contract with Troubled COVID Lab." *Cal Matters*, 1 Nov. 2021, calmatters.org. Accessed 30 Mar. 2022.

CHAPTER 5. FLATTEN THE CURVE

1. "Coronavirus, Social and Physical Distancing and Self-Quarantine." *John Hopkins Medicine*, 15 July 2020, hopkinsmedicine.org. Accessed 30 Mar. 2022.

2. Dan Mangan. "Trump Issues 'Coronavirus Guidelines' for Next 15 Days to Slow Pandemic." *CNBC*, 16 Mar. 2020, cnbc.com. Accessed 30 Mar. 2022.

3. "'Too Many People Are Dying Alone.' A New York Doctor's Story." *Rochester First*, 27 Mar. 2020, rochesterfirst.com. Accessed 30 Mar. 2022.

4. Kelly Tyko. "Target Same-Day Services Like Drive Up and Shipt Delivery Grew by 278% Fueled by COVID-19." *USA Today*, 20 May 2020, usatoday.com. Accessed 30 Mar. 2022.

5. Alina Selyukh. "Amazon Doubles Profit to $5.2 Billion as Online Shopping Spikes." *NPR*, 30 July 2020, npr.org. Accessed 30 Mar. 2022.

6. Blake Morgan. "50 Statistics Showing the Lasting Impact of COVID-19 on Consumers." *Forbes*, 19 Oct. 2020, forbes.com. Accessed 30 Mar. 2022.

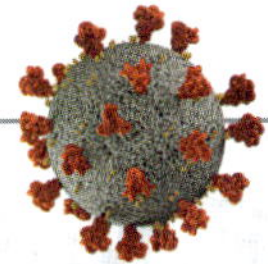

SOURCE NOTES CONTINUED

CHAPTER 6. FIGHTING FROM THE FRONT LINES

1. Adam Jeffrey and Hannah Miller. "Coronavirus: Gov. Cuomo, the National Guard and FEMA Transform the Javits Center into a Hospital." *CNBC*, 28 Mar. 2020, cnbc.com. Accessed 30 Mar. 2022.

2. Gary Hardcastle. "Every Night, New York City Salutes Its Health-Care Workers." *NPR*, 10 Apr. 2020, npr.org. Accessed 30 Mar. 2022.

3. Jamie L. LaReau. "GM and Ford End Critical Care Ventilator Production." *Detroit Free Press*, 1 Sept. 2020, freep.com. Accessed 30 Mar. 2022.

4. "Navy Hospital Ships Helping in COVID-19 Response." *US Northern Command*, 2 Apr. 2020, northcom.mil. Accessed 30 Mar. 2022.

5. Megan Eckstein. "USNS Mercy Leaves Los Angeles After Treating 77 Patients; Some Personnel Will Remain in L.A." *USNI News*, 15 May 2020, news.usni.org. Accessed 30 Mar. 2022.

6. Dakin Andone and Paul P. Murphy. "What It's Like for Health-Care Workers on the Front Lines of the Coronavirus Pandemic." *CNN*, 29 Mar. 2020, cnn.com. Accessed 30 Mar. 2022.

7. Ian Thomas. "Raising Wages Isn't Enough to Attract and Keep Workers, Experts Say." *CNBC*, 1 Sept. 2021, cnbc.com. Accessed 30 Mar. 2022.

8. Jennifer Liu. "Companies Are Planning Raises in 2022—Here's How Much Workers Can Expect." *CNBC*, 9 Dec. 2021, cnbc.com. Accessed 30 Mar. 2022.

9. Michael Corkery and Sapna Maheshwari. "Virus Cases Rise, but Hazard Pay for Retail Workers Doesn't." *New York Times*, 23 Nov. 2020, nytimes.com. Accessed 30 Mar. 2022.

CHAPTER 7. THE VACCINES

1. "Operation Warp Speed Contracts for COVID-19 Vaccines and Ancillary Vaccination Materials." *Congressional Research Service*, 1 Mar. 2021, crsreports.congress.gov. Accessed 30 Mar. 2022.

2. "COVID-19 Vaccine: What You Need to Know about the Second Dose." *MU Health Care*, 2021, muhealth.org. Accessed 30 Mar. 2022.

3. "FDA Authorizes Pfizer-BioNTech COVID-19 Vaccine for Emergency Use in Children Five through 11 Years of Age." *FDA*, 29 Oct. 2021, fda.gov. Accessed 30 Mar. 2022.

4. Colleen Moriarty. "The Link Between Myocarditis and COVID-19 mRNA Vaccines." *Yale Medicine*, 24 June 2021, yalemedicine.org. Accessed 30 Mar. 2022.

5. "Johnson & Johnson's Janssen COVID-19 Vaccine Overview and Safety." *CDC*, 22 Feb. 2022, cdc.gov. Accessed 30 Mar. 2022.

6. "Cases, Hospitalizations, and Deaths Data File." *Minnesota Department of Health*, 28 Mar. 2022, health.state.mn.us. Accessed 30 Mar. 2022.

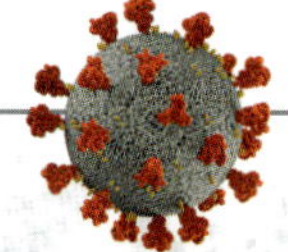

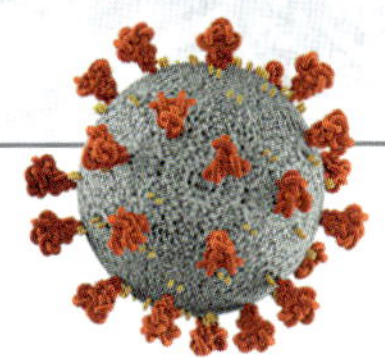
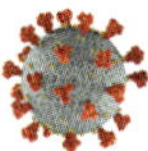

7. "COVID-19 Vaccine Booster Shots." *CDC*, 2 Feb. 2022, cdc.gov. Accessed 30 Mar. 2022.

8. Jessica Rendall. "CDC Issues New Guidance, Says Immunocompromised People Can Get 4th Shot." *CNET*, 27 Oct. 2021, cnet.com. Accessed 30 Mar. 2022.

9. "Coronavirus (COVID-19) Vaccinations." *Our World in Data*, 30 Mar. 2022, ourworldindata.org. Accessed 30 Mar. 2022.

10. "Selected Adverse Events Reported after COVID-19 Vaccination." *CDC*, 28 Mar. 2022, cdc.gov. Accessed 30 Mar. 2022.

11. "Mortality Analyses." *Johns Hopkins University & Medicine*, 30 Mar. 2022, coronavirus.jhu.edu. Accessed 30 Mar. 2022.

12. "Unvaccinated Adults Are Now More Than Three Times as Likely to Lean Republican than Democratic." *KFF*, 16 Nov. 2021, kff.org. Accessed 30 Mar. 2022.

13. "Fact Sheet: Biden Administration Announces Details of Two Major Vaccination Policies." *White House*, 4 Nov. 2021, whitehouse.gov. Accessed 30 Mar. 2022.

14. Jonathan Franklin. "10 States Sue Biden Administration over COVID Vaccine Mandate for Health-Care Workers." *NPR*, 11 Nov. 2021, npr.org. Accessed 30 Mar. 2022.

15. Melissa Quinn. "Supreme Court Blocks Biden's COVID Vaccine Rule for Companies, Allows Mandate for Health-Care Workers." *CBS News*, 14 Jan. 2022, cbsnews.com. Accessed 30 Mar. 2022.

CHAPTER 8. THE PEOPLE FIGHT THE PANDEMIC

1. Alina Selyukh. "Supermarkets Add 'Senior Hours' for Vulnerable Shoppers." *NPR*, 19 Mar. 2020, npr.org. Accessed 30 Mar. 2022.

2. Brent Schrotenboer. "Coronavirus and Shopping for Supplies: Getting to the Bottom of the Toilet Paper Shortage." *USA Today,* 8 Apr. 2020, usatoday.com. Accessed 30 Mar. 2022.

3. David Enrich, Rachel Abrams, and Steven Kurutz. "A Sewing Army, Making Masks for America." *New York Times*, 25 Mar. 2020, nytimes.com. Accessed 30 Mar. 2022.

CHAPTER 9. THE NEW NORMAL

1. Rakesh Kochhar. "Unemployment Rose Higher in Three Months of COVID-19 than It Did in Two Years of the Great Recession." *Pew Research Center*, 11 June 2020, pewresearch.org. Accessed 30 Mar. 2022.

2. "May Unemployment Stabilized or Improved in All but Three States." *USA Facts*, 19 June 2020, usafacts.org. Accessed 30 Mar. 2022.

3. Jennifer Liu. "4 Million People Quit Their Jobs in April, Sparked by Confidence They Can Find Better Work." *CNBC*, 9 June 2021, cnbc.com. Accessed 30 Mar. 2022.

4. Lauren Camera. "Schools Creep Closer to 100% Providing K–8 In-Person Instruction." *US News*, 10 June 2021, usnews.com. Accessed 30 Mar. 2022.

5. "'COVID Fatigue' Is Hitting Hard. Fighting It Is Hard, Too, Says UC Davis Health Psychologist." *UC Davis Health*, 7 July 2020, health.ucdavis.edu. Accessed 30 Mar. 2022.

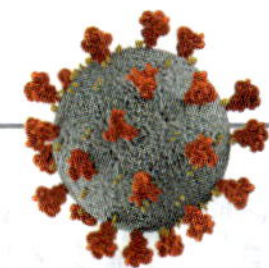

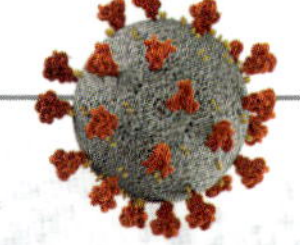

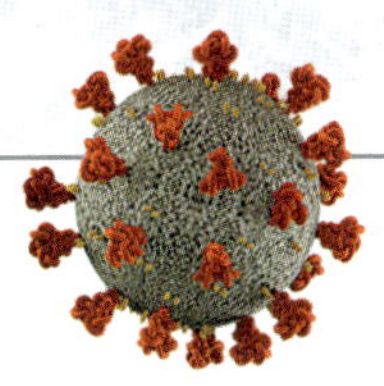
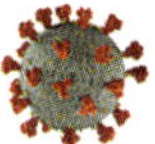

National Institutes of Health (NIH), 42, 43
New York City, 21, 27, 54, 65, 66, 70
1918 flu, 15–17, 50

Occupational Safety and Health Administration (OSHA), 86, 87
Omicron, 63, 98
Operation Warp Speed (OWS), 39, 76
outbreaks, 5–6, 8, 10, 11, 16–17, 19, 20, 21, 23–24, 30, 32, 33, 40, 43, 44–45

Path Out of the Pandemic, 41
Paul, Rand, 43
Pelosi, Nancy, 24, 37
personal protective equipment (PPE), 26–27, 60, 65, 67–68, 70
Pfizer, 76, 78–81, 84
Postmates, 62
proof of vaccination, 98, 99
public health emergency, 10, 11, 23–24

quarantine, 10, 30, 58–59, 92, 99

Redfield, Robert, 33
Republicans, 24, 36, 45, 85
Romney, Mitt, 43

schools, 6, 31, 41, 60, 62, 92, 96–97
shortages, 6, 12, 26–27, 60, 66–68, 70–71, 72, 87, 90, 91, 95–96
small businesses, 38, 41, 62
social distancing, 7, 9, 30, 32, 36, 45, 57, 77, 90, 96–97
Strategic Preparedness and Response Plan (SPRP), 30–31
symptoms, 8–9, 17, 19–20, 22, 34, 44, 47, 49, 51, 54, 58, 61, 66–67

Tedros Adhanom Ghebreyesus, 29, 30
testing, 10, 20, 24, 30, 32, 33–36, 38–39, 41–42, 43, 45, 47–55, 58, 63, 70, 72, 86, 98, 99
travel, 6, 10, 19, 22–23, 32, 33, 39, 45, 49, 59, 99

Trump, Donald, 5, 23–24, 27, 38–40, 42, 44, 60, 67, 75–76, 95
Twitter, 86

Uber Eats, 62
unemployment, 37–38, 44, 73, 95–96
United Nations, 5, 31
unvaccinated, 41, 83–84, 85, 86–87, 97

vaccines, 16–17, 33–36, 39, 42, 43, 45, 72, 75–87, 95, 96, 97–99
trials, 39, 75–76, 77
ventilators, 26–27, 66–67

wages, 72, 73, 96
Walensky, Rochelle P., 33
White House Coronavirus Task Force, 23, 38, 43
work from home, 6, 25, 62, 72, 92
World Health Organization (WHO), 5, 10, 17, 21–23, 29–31, 32, 38, 39, 43, 61

Zoom, 92

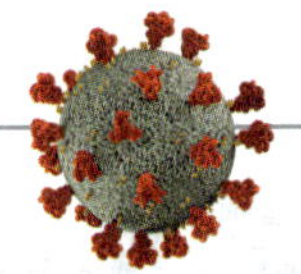

ABOUT THE AUTHOR

HEIDI DEAL

Heidi Deal is a nonfiction author specializing in science, history, and human rights.

ABOUT THE CONSULTANT

KEVIN M. BAKKER, PhD

Dr. Kevin M. Bakker's research combines field, lab, and computational components to identify and interpret the factors responsible for the complexity of ecological and epidemiological systems. He is interested in deciphering the population dynamics of infectious pathogens. Bakker has been counting SARS-CoV-2 gene copies in wastewater and has been analyzing them to understand community COVID-19 burden.

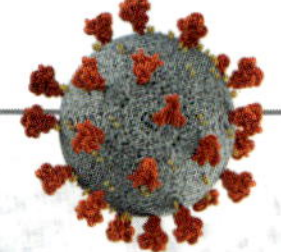